For Goodness' Sake!

For Goodness' Sake!

Growing Up in a New England Parsonage

Edith Patterson Meyer

ABINGDON PRESS
Nashville   New York

Library of Congress Cataloging in Publication Data

MEYER, EDITH PATTERSON.
For goodness' sake!
Autobiography. 1. Meyer, Edith Patterson. I. Title.
CT275.M51265A3   917.4[B]   73-6787

ISBN 0-687-13290-8

MANUFACTURED BY THE PARTHENON PRESS AT
NASHVILLE, TENNESSEE, UNITED STATES OF AMERICA

To the memory of my parents

The Reverend John Nelson Patterson
and
Etta Briant Patterson

"No truth or goodness realized by man ever dies, or can die."
—Thomas Carlyle

Pastorates of J. N. Patterson

1884–1887   Chilmark, Mass.
1887–1889   Somerset, Mass.
1889–1893   Cotuit, Mass.
1893–1897   Chatham, Mass.
1897–1899   New Bedford, Mass. (Allen Street Church)
1899–1902   Brockton, Mass. (Franklin Church)
1902–1905   Mystic and Noank, Conn.
1905–1910   Portland and South Glastonbury, Conn.
1910–1915   Thompsonville, Conn.
1915–1918   Bridgewater, Mass.
1918–1920   Fall River, Mass. (North Church)
1920–1924   Wellfleet, Mass.
1924–1928   East Wareham, Mass.

Contents

I. BABY OF THE FAMILY
  1. Another Mouth to Feed 11
  2. A-B-C's and 1-2-3's 20
  3. Island Interlude 28
  4. Time to Move 37

II. THE MIDDLE YEARS
  5. As a Family 47
  6. The Seemly Sabbath 55
  7. Double Charge 64
  8. Special Days and Holidays 73
  9. Campmeeting Vacation 82
  10. "A Penny Saved . . ." 93

11. Parsonage Guests 102
12. "In the Beginning God . . ." 111
13. Church Sociability 120
III. SPREADING WINGS
14. "And Then There Was One" 129
15. Conflicts 136
16. The Donation Party 144
17. "I Do!" 151
18. A Liberal Education 161
19. For Goodness' Sake! 170

I
Baby of the Family

1. Another Mouth to Feed

There were already four children in the family when I arrived. On the day I was born, my brothers have told me, they met in solemn conclave and decided to run away. One more mouth to feed, the three boys agreed, was going to be just too much for a poor preacher and his wife to manage. But if they—the three oldest—left home their father would have only the four-year-old sister and the new baby to provide for. That, said Walter, the oldest, should not be too great a problem.

"I'm ten," he stated grandly; "you're eight" (pointing to Herbert); "and Rob, you're seven. We're old enough to get along by ourselves. We'll start tomorrow morning before it's light, so we'll have to get our things ready now."

Walter set the example, sorting out shirts, short pants, and underwear, and Herbert and Rob followed suit. Luckily it was summer, so they could go without shoes and coats. They stacked the three piles in a corner, ready to be stuffed into their pillowcases in the morning and tied, hobo style, to three long sticks.

"Now get into bed and go to sleep," Walter directed. "I'll wake you when it's time for us to go."

Obediently Herbert and Rob climbed into the big bed. Walter blew out the light in their small lamp and crawled into the cot beside the bed. Too excited to sleep, the boys tossed and turned, then froze into sleeplike positions as they heard their father come into the room. He was carrying a lamp, and as he walked around the bed to tuck in the boy on the off side its light fell on the stacks of clothing.

Out of the corners of their nearly closed eyes the brothers watched their father clear a space on the cluttered marble-topped bureau and set down the lamp. He clasped his hands behind him in the thoughtful gesture they knew well and began to pace back and forth in the narrow space at the foot of the two beds.

Speaking softly, almost as if thinking aloud, they heard him say slowly and soberly, "God is very good to the new little girl to put her in a home with three big brothers. They will be a great help in bringing her up. In fact"—he paused a moment—"I don't know how their mother and I could ever manage without them." The three boys stirred uncomfortably. "We've a wonderful family now," their father went on. "Three fine boys and two lovely little girls." He picked up the lamp. "Good night, boys," he whispered. "God give you good sleep." And he went out, closing the door gently behind him.

Walter was the first to speak. "I guess we can't do it," he said uncertainly. "You heard what Father said. They're counting on us. I guess we'll have to stay." After a moment of thoughtful silence he announced, "I know what I can do. First thing tomorrow I'm going down to Old Man Nickerson's and get a job helping him haul lobster pots."

"I heard they needed a delivery boy at Ellises," Herbert spoke up. "I'll go there and see if they'll take me."

"What can I do?" wailed Rob. "I can do something. I'm nearly eight."

"We'll find a job for you," Walter promised. "Now"—firmly—

12

"you kids go to sleep. And when you get up in the morning put away your clothes. Father was right. We belong here."

"Here" was a Methodist parsonage in the small town at the "elbow" of Cape Cod. It was a healthy, friendly place for a growing family, with a large yard, space for a garden, and the old white church just a few steps down the hill. Yet almost before I could toddle (though not before I had inhaled a lifelong love of salt air) the setting changed, in the manner of the Methodist ministry at the turn of the century. At the annual spring conference Father was appointed to serve a church in the seaport city of New Bedford.

This parsonage was small and compact, hardly big enough for the large family, and set in a handkerchief patch of lawn behind a picket fence. House and pickets were painted a dull brown, as was the nearby church. The color was no doubt carefully chosen for reasons of economy and durability, but it was depressing. Though I was under four when we moved again, one of the few things I remembered about that home was the dreary brown paint.

A fair amount of horse-drawn traffic passed along the street in front, and at three my interest in the Great Unknown beyond the fence compelled my parents to tether me like a calf in the small yard. I resented the humiliating rope, and whenever I heard the gate latch click as someone entered or left the yard I would strain at my tether to catch a wider view of the tantalizing world beyond.

My unhappiness over the confining rope eventually persuaded my parents to remove it on my solemn promise not to go out of the gate. At three I knew well enough the meaning of obedience and disobedience and the unpleasant consequences connected with the latter. I would keep my promise not to go out of the gate. But nothing had been said about the fence. Stealthily I dragged a chair out of the kitchen, tumbled it down the back steps, pulled it across the little lawn, and set it against the fence. Climbing up on it and then onto the narrow rail near the top of the pickets, I lifted first one foot and then the other over them and cautiously slid down the outside of the fence. I laughed aloud. I was free— free to explore the fascinating outside world! And I had not broken my promise. Down the street I ran as fast as my feet would carry me.

My excursion was a brief one. Someone soon spotted my absence and the telltale chair beside the fence. Before I reached the first cross street I was captured and firmly escorted back inside the fence, by way of the gate. But I did not suffer the usual punishment for disobedience—a spanking. My parents had a very real sense of justice and they could not dispute my words, drawled in the slow way I am told I first talked: "I didn't go through the gate. I went over the fence." Since evasiveness seemed too difficult a concept to explain to a three-year-old, they compromised by extracting from me another promise, this one including the fence.

Church and home; home and church. These were the two focal points about which my parents'—and, by extension, their children's—lives revolved. For my father it was in the first order; for my mother, the second. The ministry was not a profession to my father; it was a "calling." He felt he had definitely been "called" to win souls to Christ and to help establish God's kingdom on earth. The area touched by the church to which he had been appointed as spiritual leader was his special responsibility, and to this commission he devoted himself wholeheartedly. With deep sincerity he extended his religious zeal to his personal life and to his home, striving to make them both exemplary.

My mother was by nature more of a Martha than a Mary. She expressed her religious devotion by using her considerable administrative talents both in the home and in church activities. Somehow she found time and energy not only to manage her large household skillfully on an extremely small budget but also to participate actively in church affairs. Probably she spent less time in the kitchen than most mothers of five growing children, but she prided herself on being a good "plain" cook and on serving her family nourishing low-cost meals.

My brothers' forebodings that with a fifth child in the household there would not be enough food to go around never, thank goodness, came true. If we did not know the taste of steak, the Saturday-Sunday pot roast and the midweek stew, beef loaf, and vegetable soup with its meaty bone were satisfying and tasty. The vitamins we had not heard of were supplied in summer from the large garden tended by Father and in winter from the cellar shelves of home-canned fruits and vegetables put up by Mother.

Plain, healthful food, a sound education, and conscientious religious and ethical training were what my parents considered essential for their children. They would make their home a good

14

one by welcoming to it whatever might contribute to the development of sturdy bodies and minds and Christian character. In due time, God willing, their children should go out into the world as strong, clear-thinking men and women, equipped to meet the challenge of life and to do their share toward shaping a better world.

Training began early. A child could scarcely be too young, both parents believed, to be taught the difference between right and wrong and the obligation to choose the right. Not only was this necessary for the child's development but it was important so that the minister's family might serve as an example in the community. Other children must never be able to excuse a misdeed by saying, "But one of the minister's children did it, so why can't I?" "It will not be hard to be an example," our father said repeatedly, "if you just remember to do what you know is right."

Each morning family prayers followed the hearty breakfast as regularly as it, preceded by a brief blessing, followed the night of sleep. Before I could walk I was held, squirming, on my mother's lap while my father read a fairly long passage from the Bible. When he knelt to pray Mother put me on my knees beside her where I fidgeted until, at the close of his prayer the kneeling family repeated together the Lord's Prayer.

Morning devotions over, the parsonage throbbed with bustle and stir. The four oldest children readied themselves for school, were inspected by Mother for cleanliness and neatness, then rushed away. Without a moment's rest she and the "hired girl" tackled the household tasks, beginning with the breakfast dishes. I tagged after them as they made the beds, tidied the house, and started the dinner. Having a helper was something my mother insisted on, though my father, rather minimizing the work of running a household, considered the two dollars—sometimes three—a week plus food and lodging a rather unnecessary burden on the family exchequer. Of course every child also had daily chores to do; long before school days I learned to wipe the silverware and set the table.

"No time for dawdling!" was one of Mother's favorite remarks, and certainly she was no dawdler. She worked energetically, efficiently, and with one eye on the clock. Doing the necessary domestic tasks, she believed, should precede any really enjoyable activity. "First work, then play." Yet she made a sort of game of much of her work, with time as her opponent. She would try to finish this or that task by a certain quarter-hour, or to beat her own record in ironing a tablecloth or my father's stiffly starched "pulpit" shirt.

Sewing and mending, which Mother enjoyed more than cooking or cleaning, were reserved for afternoon. With dinner over and the older children back at school she would allow herself the luxury of a short nap before, at two-thirty, donning an afternoon dress and a fancy white apron, she would seat herself in her favorite wicker rocking chair next to the large and always overloaded sewing basket.

My nap over, I would sit beside her in my little rocker and listen delightedly to her stories of "when I was a little girl in New Jersey." I liked best those about her childhood visits to her grand-father's—how she sat in front of him when he rode horseback over his big farm; how her uncles made her the doll cradle that was now mine; how she wept when the farm dog she loved died and her uncles would not let her go with them to bury him; and how she watched her grandmother make up packages to send one of the uncles who went away to the war in the South.

Who knows how many short pants were patched or long black stockings darned during those pleasant afternoon sessions? Clothes might be handed down, made over, or not of the best quality, but they were always well mended, clean, and respectable looking. My father, I am sure, had no idea what a godsend my mother's fondness for sewing was. Clothing three growing boys and two growing girls on a minister's salary, before the days of inexpensive ready-made garments, was a constant struggle.

My brothers did not forget their resolve to help bring up the baby of the family. They often brought me little trifles to treasure and took time to talk to me on my level of understanding and to play with me in an offhand, big-brotherly manner. Sometimes this involved a bit of teasing which might be cut short by a parent's admonition: "Go easy; your little sister isn't old enough to appreciate that kind of fun."

My father too enjoyed playing with me. As a tiny child I would squeal with delight as he played patty-cake with me, or tossed me up in his arms, or let me climb over him as he stretched out on the floor. A special treat was his jogging me on his knee to the tune of "Master Blacksmith, fellow fine/Will you shoe this horse of mine?/Here a nail and there a prod (pressing his forefinger against the bare sole of my small foot)/And *that* horse is well shod!"

My sister Helen, having been the only girl and the youngest of the family for four years prior to my appearance, must have found me a little hard to take. I know she disliked our being lumped together as "the girls," for although we shared the same bed and did various household tasks together the four-year difference in our ages made our interests too unlike for close companionship. She was a leader, and I was not a follower. All through childhood we had spirited scuffles and hair-pullings which often resulted in the application of the back of a hairbrush to the back of the person, both hers and mine.

Being the only one not yet in school, I was frequently taken by my mother to meetings at the church and in various homes. At these Ladies Aid sewing circles, gatherings of ministers and their wives, missionary and temperance programs, I was usually allowed to wander around and explore things that interested me, always provided I did not touch and was quiet. The ladies made much of me and I appreciated the cookies and cakes they gave me; they were fancier than those I got at home. But on the way back to the parsonage—I suppose to counteract any possible spoiling—Mother almost always rather took the edge off my pleasure by mentioning something I had said or done which was "not quite befitting a little lady and a minister's daughter." Unless I behaved better next time, the implication was clear, these enjoyable excursions might have to be curtailed.

My father, while obviously proud of his three active sons, was a far firmer disciplinarian with them than with his two younger daughters. Yet he allowed them considerable freedom and showed real respect for their individual personalities. Each boy was encouraged to plan his own activities; each had his own possessions and any borrowing must be done with the owner's consent; each boy must show reasonable consideration for the others.

To protect their independence and privacy one of the boys printed the letters M—Y—O—B on a large cardboard and placed it in a prominent position near the dining-room table. If during a meal someone asked a too-personal question the boy involved would point silently but eloquently to the sign to remind the questioner to Mind Your Own Business.

A sort of "All for one; one for all" understanding prevailed among the boys; when urged to "go outside and work off your animal spirits" they usually did so as a group. They knew that all wrestling, tussling, and rough-housing must be done out of doors. Inside, Mother encouraged quiet pastimes over noisy fun, partly to save nerves but more, no doubt, to save wear and tear on the church-owned furniture.

Helen and I often envied our brothers' greater freedom. Our parents seemed to assume that girls had fewer "animal spirits," and we were frequently reminded to be "ladylike." One thing we definitely resented was being expected to tidy up the house after our brothers and help keep it always "presentable" for unexpected callers.

Much as every child's individual projects were encouraged, they did not take the place of family activities. A mile or two away from the brown house in the city was a delightful little park where in warm weather we sometimes ate a picnic supper. To get there, Helen would ride for half fare with Mother on the trolley or streetcar (which we also called the "electric"). The boys would go on the bicycles which they were buying with proceeds from the newspaper routes which each of them had. Father also rode a bicycle, and I rode with him on a little seat he had contrived, securely fastened to the handlebars. While my mother and sister spread the supper on a red-checked tablecloth in the small picnic area shaded by plane trees (locally known as buttonwoods), I ran about on the grass. Nearby my father and brothers would toss around a ball. When my brothers treated me to a little ride in an old rowboat tied at the edge of the park's small pond, I was so delighted that I headed for the pond again, hoping to repeat the experience by myself. On being dragged back I stamped my foot rebelliously, shouting, "I'm a-doin' in dat boat!" I did not achieve my ambition, but I did provide the family with a handy slogan to use when one's heart was set on some particular project.

My father and I were the best of companions. Occasionally when he made an afternoon round of calls on shut-ins he would take me along, perched before him on his bicycle. I loved the swift motion of the wheel, the close companionship of my father, and the parishioners' petting. I knew that during the calls I must not fidget too much, I should speak only when spoken to, and I must kneel quietly for the prayer with which my father almost always ended his call. Once I slipped. When calling on someone who had previously given me a cookie I sniffed audibly and inquired politely, "Do I smell cookies?" Then quickly recovering myself I remarked, "I didn't ask for any, did I!"

Often before settling down to a morning's work Father would pace the study floor doing vocal exercises to strengthen his voice. Inhaling deeply he would enunciate: "*a—e—i—o—u.*" I loved to follow behind him doing my best to emulate him by loudly mouthing the vowels after him. I liked to follow him too when he put on old clothes and went out to work in the vegetable garden or to the backyard woodpile where he sawed long logs into shorter, stove lengths. He had grown up on a farm and enjoyed outdoor work. He said it cleared his brain and was the start of many a sermon; it was also a great help financially. Often he would whistle as he worked. Or he might sing in his pleasant baritone voice—usually hymns, but also old Scottish songs learned, he said, from his Scotch-Irish father. He would have been surprised at the mental picture I had when he sang "The Campbells Are Coming"—a procession of camels crossing a desert!

Although Father's bicycle was his trusty steed, he was a great walker. For short distances, and sometimes for longer ones, he often preferred "shanks' mare." Even as a tiny girl I loved to walk beside him, holding his hand tightly and trying to keep up with him. At first he would shorten his steps, then he would become immersed in thought and forgetting me would stride out until I was fairly running beside him. Suddenly remembering me, he would readjust his pace—and so it would go.

No matter what the pace, I was proud and happy to walk beside this tall, dignified man with the kind face and the far-seeing, often twinkling blue eyes. I liked it when he stopped to shake hands with someone we met and to inquire warmly after his or her well-being and that of the family. I was conscious of the pleasant, rather restrained greetings of shopkeepers and others which somehow indicated the high esteem in which they held "the parson." Basking in reflected glory, I thoroughly enjoyed being a minister's daughter.

2. A-B-C's and 1-2-3's

Much of the "busy work" my ex-teacher mother provided for me in my preschool days had definite educational values, though the term "educational toy" was not then in general use. Stringing buttons, she believed, was both fun and a good way to train eye and hand. By selecting from the big box half-filled with buttons of all shapes and sizes those of the same color or size and threading them on a long string I had the fun—and sense of accomplishment —of making myself a necklace. When I tired of wearing it I had only to break the string and let the buttons fall back into the big box.

A set of stencil cards holding outlines of animals and birds (somewhat blurred from being used by four sets of hands before mine) introduced me to these creatures and strengthened finger muscles. Another enjoyable and educational project was spool-knitting. Here I could create play reins by twisting bright-colored yarn about brads nailed onto the top of an empty spool and pulling it through the hole.

Dressing and undressing dolls was a favorite pastime, especially since Helen provided me with a variety of doll clothes made out of discarded materials stashed away in Mother's flour-sack scrap-bag. When some small neighbor came to play with me we would treat my family of dolls—and ourselves—to a tea party, using a set of doll dishes that had been Mother's. Making believe we were grown-ups we would carry on pretend conversations; drink pretend tea; and eat not pretend but real cookies, sugar or molasses, fresh from the cookie jar.

But what I liked best was playing with the big box of blocks which a wealthy parishioner had sent to the parsonage one Christmas before I was born. Not a block was missing in spite of its having seen almost daily service for many years, due to Mother's strict rule that all blocks must be replaced after every play session with them. Putting back the top layer of irregularly shaped blocks was not only fun but a task which helped develop concepts of size and shape. These blocks provided hours of happy play for all the children. Even when the boys were half grown they enjoyed helping their younger sisters raise towers, build castles and forts, and line up rows of blocks to be toppled with a gentle nudge.

At four I realized that reading played a large part in the life of everyone around me. I resented that I was the only one left out of this seemingly fascinating occupation. Why couldn't I make sense out of those strange marks on the pages of books and magazines?

My parents had no compunctions about preschool children learning to read. They were proud of the fact that every child of theirs was able to read before entering school. When my brothers were small my father had painstakingly hand-printed simple words and short sentences in large clear letters on a dozen or so white pages. These my mother made into a book by stitching them to-gether on her sewing machine. Now this homemade pre-primer was resurrected for my use. Every day my father found time to hold me in his lap and read aloud the letters and words while I followed along with my small forefinger held under his larger one.

At mealtimes I was allowed to use a special plate which had the letters of the alphabet ranged around the rim, circling a Mother Goose picture. Motivated by the plate, the pre-primer, and my eager desire to read, the day arrived, well before my fifth birthday, when I suddenly shouted, "I can read!"

I remember the moment well. I was sitting on the floor in my favorite bay-window nook. In my hand was a book; I believe it was the *Hiawatha Primer* outgrown by my sister and taken over by me. All at once the symbols on the page made sense. They said something! They spoke to me! And the mystery of reading began to clear away. Nearly beside myself with joy I danced about the room, then ran to demonstrate my newfound skill to anyone I could find. Now I would no longer be the "baby"—a term I resented fiercely. Now I would be a real member of the family and the equal of my sister—or nearly.

About this same time I began to get meaning from spelled-out words. "I plan to go d-o-w-n-t-o-w-n and take E-d-i-t-h with me," I heard my mother say one day. "Goody! I'm going downtown!" I squealed. From then on everyone knew it was useless to spell out words not intended for "little Edie's" ears.

Numbers I found much harder to understand than letters. Why one and one should want to get together and make two I couldn't imagine, even a long time after I was reading simple sentences with ease. The days of the month were a mystery too, and when on the first day of the new month I saw my sister going around tearing a leaf off the calendar which hung in almost every room I followed suit. As my mother pinned back the detached leaves she tried to explain to me about the months with their quota of days. I was still bewildered, though pleased with her promise that when the next month came round I would be allowed to take off the top leaves from the calendars.

If I could only go to school I was sure I could soon solve all the mysteries, both of letters and of numbers. Besides, it was lonesome to be at home all day when all the other children were at school. "Next year," I was told. "This year you are not quite old enough."

"But I can read better than some of my friends in the first grade," I protested, and it was true.

"I wish there were a public kindergarten," my mother sighed. But there was not.

Each morning I moped about as my brothers and sister started for school, then went to sit by the window to watch enviously as groups of smaller children went by on their way to the school for the lower grades, which was only a block away. In vain did my father try to raise my spirits by spending more time with me over the pages of the little primer and my sister's outgrown readers. It was school I wanted, and nothing else would satisfy. Finally my parents paid a visit to the authorities and gained their consent to let me try the first grade on a sort of probationary basis.

Joining the other children on the short walk to school, having a desk to sit at, colored crayons to draw with, and a blackboard to look at spelled heaven to me. I took like a duck to water to reading, spelling, and writing, but not to "number work." There I floundered about until I discovered that the teacher wrote the numbers on the board in a certain order. She wrote $1 + 1 = ?$ $2 + 1 = ?$ $3 + 1 = ?$ and the number she wanted to replace the question mark was always the number that followed it! For a few days number work was simple. Then, alas, the teacher changed the order. With the pattern gone I was sunk. I wept, fearing that my days in first grade might be ended. When I explained the difficulty to my mother she, having once been a first-grade teacher herself, taught me what I had not been able to learn in school.

Now all was well. I was no longer on probation but an accepted first-grade pupil, an honest-to-goodness schoolgirl! One look at my beaming face and my father said, "Her cup runneth over." What cup, I wondered. This, I suspected, was something I would not learn in first grade. Perhaps after all one did not learn everything in school. It might be harder than I thought to catch up with Helen and my brothers, but I would keep on trying! I wanted so much to understand everything they said and did so that I would belong to the family as an equal, not just as "the baby."

The city of Brockton, Massachusetts, where we now lived, was an industrial one concentrating largely on shoemaking. It had a big Irish-American population, and some of these families lived not far from our neighborhood. My brothers liked to play hockey with a group of the Irish boys. My mother objected; she called the boys "toughies" and disliked having her sons associate with them. The real reason, my brothers claimed, was that they were Roman Catholics. Religious prejudice was not frowned on in those pre-ecumenical days, and Irish Catholics were especially discriminated against by Protestants. This was partly because of their religion but also because of the widely held belief that they came from a crude and poverty-stricken land. My parents accepted the fact that their children's schoolmates would come from all types of homes and all kinds of religious backgrounds, but they preferred that their children choose their playmates and companions from Protestant families, preferably Methodist, of course. Unitarians and Roman Catholics were to be treated courteously but coolly.

When a substitute player was needed for the neighborhood hockey game and in desperation the boys invited Helen to fill in, Mother refused to let her play. Hockey was too rough a sport for a girl, she said, and did not become a minister's daughter. But my brothers believed it was not the game but the company that she objected to.

Occasionally my brothers and sister put on a show in the rather large basement of our house, for which admission was charged in pins. The "kids" of the neighborhood, including some of the Irish boys and girls, came and sat on planks stretched between boxes. I was pleased to be asked to be Little Miss Muffet in a shadow play. I had no difficulty in screaming and dropping my wooden bowl when a realistic paper spider was led down on a string before me, or in coming out from behind the sheet and reciting the verse.

A few days later a group of the older boys and girls who had attended the show "captured" me as a "hostage" in an Indian game they were playing. I was badly frightened and longed for one of my big brothers to appear and rescue me. Then, to my relief, I was told that I could win my release by reciting Little Miss Muffet and counting to a hundred. When I did both, my captors kept their promise and let me go. I hastily headed for home, still shaking but feeling somehow victorious and convinced that knowledge was power.

Every evening from Monday through Friday homework hour began as soon as the supper dishes were done. While Father worked in his study or was away attending some meeting and Mother busied herself with her interminable sewing or with planning some church activity, the house assumed an unnatural air of quiet. The center of the scene was the dining-room table, with the overhead hanging lamp pulled low for maximum light.

Four heads bent over four different school assignments while the first-grader struggled with one of Helen's old readers. Concentration was something none of these five children would need to learn in later life; it was absorbed in those week-night hours around the dining-room table. As soon as anyone finished his work he was free to leave the group, but quiet must be maintained for the whole sixty-minute period, unless the last one had finished his work before its end.

The charm of school did not wear off for me when, before the end of my first full school year, we moved from the Massachusetts city to a small Connecticut town. The wooden school building which housed the first few grades was something like a country school, with two grades occupying each room. I was put in the second grade but humiliatingly had to do my number work with the first grade.

The school day here began with the recitation of the Lord's Prayer, followed by the children reciting in unison a curious sort of alphabetical arrangement of proverbs and precepts. *A* stood for "A stitch in time saves nine"; *B* for "Be good to one another"; *C* was "Count your blessings"; and *D,* "Dare to do right." Each day a new quotation was added until, presumably, all twenty-six letters were covered. I still wonder what some of the other precepts were, and whether the teacher concocted this moral-training alphabet herself or used some prearranged list.

This school was farther from home than the city school had been, but I did not mind the walk along a pleasant residential street with large houses set back in lawns adorned with trees and blossoming shrubs and with flower-bordered paths leading to the front and side doors. It was fun in the autumn to shuffle through bright-colored leaves fallen from the great maples and elms overhead and to smell the tangy aroma of carefully supervised bonfires.

On the first snowy day of winter my parents thought the sidewalks would not be cleared before schooltime and my father offered to "play horse" and pull me to school on my sled. Plowing through the several inches of new-fallen snow was exciting, but I never wanted the experience repeated for I was the only one to arrive at school in this fashion. Boys and girls, I soon discovered, were expected to walk through the snow to school, and I learned that most fathers were not free at this hour to haul their children on sleds.

Reading became a passion with me. I filched a third-grade reader from someone's desk and slyly took it home overnight. Later I did the same with a fourth-grade one. I pestered every member of my family to let me read aloud to them, occasionally asking their help with an unfamiliar word. Any book or magazine lying around I would pick up and try to decipher.

There was no lack of reading matter for me to try my skill on, for in our home books and magazines were considered as essential as food and clothing. In addition to the daily newspaper, each week brought two church papers. These were scanned by my father and read more carefully by my mother, who relayed to him anything of importance which she thought he might have missed. When Father noted some book he believed would build up his theological library or be of practical help to him in his work, he first considered the price, then perhaps sent for it. At the annual Methodist church conference which he attended along with all the other Methodist ministers of the area he carefully examined the books on display and ordered several. The arrival of the box of books was an event we all anticipated. We stood around to watch as Father opened the box and took out the books one by one. Though they were completely unintelligible to me I looked them over carefully, feeling a companionable understanding of my father's deep affection for books.

Except for necessary schoolbooks not many books were purchased for the rest of the family. They were borrowed from the Sunday-school library, the town library, and from friends. Each week *The Youths' Companion* arrived and was fought over for first possession, then eventually read practically cover to cover by several pairs of eyes. From the rather nondescript Sunday-school library I took home many books, including the "Pansy" and "Dotty Dimple" series. The "Five Little Peppers" and the "Little Colonel" books I borrowed from somewhere and read with delight, sharing parts of them with my mother while she mended or sewed. For a time she was concerned about my great love of fairy tales, but she did not forbid them and my reading interests soon widened. In fact, almost anything in print was acceptable to me; I was not critical, and my appetite for reading was practically insatiable.

It annoyed me that I was not yet allowed to take my turn at the family read-aloud sessions, which occurred on those rare evenings when my father was home and free for an hour. Among the books we heard were Hawthorne's *Twice Told Tales, Beside the Bonny Brier Bush, Cranford, Picciola,* and many of Tolstoi's short stories. My mother did most of the reading, with Helen spelling her for short stretches. Father would pace up and down listening intently, while my brothers would listen "with one ear" as they worked on a puzzle or perhaps fairly noiselessly whittled out some small object. Helen, who enjoyed sewing, might work on a piece of needlework or on making a doll dress for me. I, who detested sewing, might try to complete my daily stint of a square of patchwork, periodically pricking myself, knotting my thread, or losing my needle.

Occasionally Father would stop the reading to straighten out some point he felt was not clear or to settle some question, perhaps of pronunciation, with the aid of the dictionary or encyclopedia. When he did this my mother would protest, "We'll lose the thread of the story," or "We'll never finish this book if you insist on stopping." She liked to get ahead with the reading and had a pleasant sense of accomplishment when the bookmark was set ahead by a chapter or two or a sizable number of pages. But Father would have his way, insisting that it was important to clear up any possible misconception "here and now."

Most of the classics or near-classics selected for those read-aloud sessions might be considered beyond the level of understanding of a small girl. Yet I cannot remember ever being bored, and frequently the beauty of the language as well as much of the story came through to me. Often a strange word or expression would catch my fancy so that I would inquire about it later. Sometimes too the impact of a story would be so strong that I would mull it over for days and the impression would linger, though perhaps faintly, for years.

3. Island Interlude

The first year of Father's pastorate in New Bedford the family discovered that summer there was far different from summer on the Cape. No air conditioners existed to cool the house, and the outdoor air was often stifling. The "baby of the family" was seeming to wilt under the heat. "Edith is getting puny," her mother said. "I'm worried about her." She worried too about the empty days for the rest of the children. She did not wholly approve of the boys' new playmates; there were no supervised playgrounds or other wholesome play opportunities available and, except for their newspaper routes, the boys were still too young to look for jobs. The family, she and Father decided, simply must not spend the long school vacation in the hot city. But what could be done? The almost hand-to-mouth budget included no vacation fund.

In a moment of inspiration the parents thought of the nearby island of Martha's Vineyard. The minister-father's first pastorate had been in the little community of Chilmark, "up-island." It was there that he had taken his New Jersey bride and welcomed his first two sons. There, as in every place they had lived, he and his wife still had warm friends. Mother wrote to one of them, a sea captain's widow, inquiring if she might happen to know of a vacant house available at low cost for the summer months. In reply the generous woman offered without charge her own roomy farmhouse; she could move in with a son's family where she spent much of her time anyway. Her house had no "modern conveniences," but she believed it would be adequate for the family and that the children would enjoy playing in the large yard and empty barn.

What a friend! And what a happy solution to the worrisome problem! So on a Monday morning in late June the family of seven, loaded to the eyebrows, set out for their Martha's Vineyard vacation. They boarded the steamer which made the trip across Buzzards Bay daily, and piled their loads on a bench selected to serve as headquarters for the trip. The boys began their excited exploration of the ship, leaving their father with Helen in tow far behind, while their unsealoving mother and her youngest remained on the sheltered bench. To her delight puny "little Edie" seemed to perk up with the first sea breeze, and when the family assembled at noon to eat the hearty lunch packed in the cream-o'-wheat boxes she showed an appetite lacking for weeks.

The generous widow had driven a farm wagon down to meet the boat. She saw to the loading of the luggage in the back of the wagon, motioned the parson and his wife to the high seat in front and helped the children scramble into the back. There, nestled among the suitcases, bags, bundles, and wraps, they sniffed the invigorating sea air and gazed at the unspoiled countryside as the old horse carried them steadily up-island.

At the farm the boys raced about, enjoying a freedom they could not know in their city home. The yard was large enough for all sorts of games, and the barn with its empty hayloft was ideal for rainy days. Low stone walls, hung with raspberry and blackberry vines, separated the farmstead from the surrounding meadows, which invited exploration, running, ball-throwing, and—later in the summer—berrypicking. Beyond the meadows lay hilly pastures with moving white objects that turned out to be sheep.

In the house the big kitchen with its well-scoured wooden floor, its wood-burning range, pine table, and sturdy chairs became the center of family life. There was also a sitting room and a carpeted, cluttered parlor which Mother promptly declared out of bounds for fear harm might come to some treasure. The upstairs held enough airy bedrooms to take care of everyone.

Facilities were primitive—no running water and an outside privy. But no one expected a bathroom in a farmhouse, and not far away in a brook with stepping stones was a small dammed-up pool where one could dip in a pail and bring it up full of clear spring water. The old-fashioned stove, Mother soon discovered, would work—as it had done for years.

The nearest neighbor was a quarter of a mile away and the little country store a mile and a half—just a good hike for the boys, our fond-of-walking father remarked. But he promised to see to laying in a supply of groceries before he left to go back to his duties in the city, and he would arrange for the use of a horse and wagon during the visits he hoped to make every second or third midweek. Perhaps the horse and conveyance could also be used to take the family on outings!

Even before he went back to the city on Friday the family was happily settled in the farmhouse, and our efficient mother was adjusted to running her household in someone else's home. She worked out a daily routine, assigning tasks to each member of the family. One of the boys' regular chores was to carry several buckets of water each morning from the spring to the kitchen. Helen helped do the dishes, make the beds, tidy the house, and peel potatoes. I was still a little young to be of much assistance, but Mother soon found simple things for me to do. Once a week everybody pitched in to help with the family wash. Because of Mother's skillful organization, as well as the simpler way of life —going barefoot, wearing old clothes and few of them, eating meals picnic style—most of the day was free for outdoor fun.

The three boys found many things with which to occupy themselves. They had read of cairns and determined to erect one on each of the several low hills visible from the farm. Taking their lunch, with each boy packing his own, they hiked across pastures to distant hilltops where they gathered stones and heaped them in a pile to begin their cairn. On later trips they added more stones until finally the hilltop piles were high enough to be seen from some distance away.

In a small patch of woods a mile or so from the farm the boys built a little hut and dammed up the small stream which flowed beside it to make a swimming pool. In spite of the icy coldness of the water they considered it fun to dip into it bareskinned. The hut and the swimming pool were the boys' exclusive domain; they bragged much about it but strictly barred their mother and sisters from it.

They did concede that the family might have a Fourth of July picnic beside "their" stream. Father unfortunately had to be in the city on that day but Mother promised to think of some way to make it special. What she contrived first sent the boys searching for thin pieces of wood and then whittling them into boat shapes, sharply pointed at the front end and with a hole bored in it to attach a long piece of string. On the miniature boats she marked places where empty spools (which were never thrown away) were to be tacked. The hole in these spool smokestacks, she explained, was just the right size to hold a small firecracker, and she gave the boys a few pennies to hike over to the country store and purchase a limited supply of them.

On the big day we carried our picnic lunch, and the boys their boats, to the edge of the wood, where we dumped our loads beneath a tree overhanging the stream. The boys lighted the fire-crackers neatly fitted into the spool smokestacks and, each holding the end of the long string attached to his boat, set the miniature battleships afloat. After a moment of suspense the naval battle began with the loud *pop, pop, pop* of the firecrackers. With each explosion the ships swirled, tossed about, and bumped into one another. When the din subsided the boys retrieved their ships by the long strings, reloaded and refired them, and sent them out to sea for another exciting naval battle. By the time the supply of firecrackers was exhausted everyone was ready for the picnic lunch, made up of family favorites. Altogether, all agreed that the holiday was a satisfying and rather special one.

Each time Father came for a midweek visit we had an all-day outing, usually at the beach. One or two of the boys would go with him to the farm where he had arranged to get a horse and wagon. Outside our farmhouse kitchen door we would load the wagon with old wraps, towels, an umbrella to protect Mother from the sun, and the lunch—especially the lunch. Under our old clothes we wore bathing suits.

We rode for several miles along dusty, bumpy country roads with Father driving, of course. At the brow of the little hill that led down to the wide beach, tall trees arched over the road, making a kind of green tunnel through which one could glimpse the water beyond. I watched eagerly for this point and loved the first sight of the blue ocean seen through the screen of green. Then the wagon rattled down the hill and onto the sand, and the journey was over. We children jumped out and, while Father tied the horse in a shady spot, peeled off our clothes and, clad in our ample bathing suits, scampered for the water. I liked chasing the waves along the shore but even better I liked squatting in the little pools left by the receding tide. Sitting in the tepid salty water seemed to me like being in a tiny private bathtub all my own.

Occasionally instead of going to this quiet beach where the sea was calm and safe and few people ever came, we would drive to the other side of the island, where the surf pounded in and the breakers were noisy and high. At this beach a row of bathhouses stood against a high bluff, facing the ocean. Mother had been given the key to one of them and we took turns using it. On my first sight of the breaking surf from the top of the bluff my mother said I clapped my hands and shouted, "Oh, see the pretty ruffles!" Whereupon, for awhile, the breakers became "ruffles" to the whole family.

Everyone slid down the bluff to the beach below. There were no lifesavers, and because of the dangerous undertow no one went out very far. My brothers were not allowed to go beyond where Father ventured. Mother, being unable to swim and not overfond of the water, stayed close to shore with Helen and me. We skipped about in the breaking waves and chased them as they rolled up on the sand.

One all-day outing took us not to the shore but to a clearing in a stretch of woodland. A few years earlier it had been set afire by lightning and where the underbrush had burned, blueberry bushes had grown up. During the berry season the area was literally blue with huge, beautiful berries.

For this berry-picking picnic we had joined the family of a Methodist minister who served a church farther down on the island. The children were more or less our ages, and they led the way up the woodland trail from the place where the horses and wagons had been left. Each of us carried empty baskets and tin pails, leaving our parents to bring the joint picnic lunch.

Blueberry bushes were everywhere, and all of them were loaded with the luscious berries. In no time all containers were filled to the brim—and so were our stomachs. Yet we willingly sat down to the combined picnic fare. The other minister's wife had brought a pie—blueberry, of course—but before it was time to cut it a horrified cry went up: "Chauncey's sat on the pie!" One look at the back side of Chauncey's short pants testified to the truth of the statement. Luckily, his mother consoled herself, they were his oldest pair. But there was no blueberry pie for dessert, and for the rest of the day Chauncey wore very peculiar-looking pants.

During the time when berries were ripe they formed a substantial part of the family diet. Even for children made hungry by much activity in sun-salty country air, blackberries, blueberries, huckleberries, or raspberries could make the better part of a satisfying meal. We had them with cereal and milk for breakfast, as pudding or cake—rarely pie—at the hearty noon meal, and great dishes of them for supper, accompanied by fresh milk and plentiful slices of buttered homemade bread. It was the rule that each youngster must provide his own berries, plus a few extra for Mother. No one had to go far to find them, and usually one could take one's choice of red or black raspberries, thimble-sized blackberries, tough-skinned huckleberries, or blueberries the size of small grapes.

On Sundays our mother led her brood to the little country church a mile away. We might follow the dusty country road, or in fine dry weather we might take a shortcut across pastures and meadows. This involved going over a couple of stiles and climbing several low stone walls, some of them entwined with fragrant wild roses. It was not easy on this cross-country walk to keep one's Sunday clothes intact, with no brier tears or berry or grasshopper stains.

The morning service seemed extra long and confining after the week's freedom, but we were frequently rewarded by being invited to some kind person's home for Sunday dinner. This was likely to feature fish or clam chowder followed by heaping plates of chicken and potatoes with gravy, and homemade pie.

On one of those Sunday visits an old sea captain let me look through his spyglass. To my astonishment I saw a sailing vessel far out at sea as clearly as if it had been in the captain's front yard. I listened eagerly as he regaled the boys with tales of his years at sea. One of them involved the drowning of several men. What drowning was I didn't know, but I deduced it was something unpleasant which could happen to people who fell into water. So it was not surprising that when I lost my balance on the stepping stones of the little brook where our drinking water came from I sat waist-deep in the cold water howling, "I'm drowned! I'm drowned!" A quick run to the house, a rubdown and dry clothes, and a few comforting words from my mother managed to restore my composure and convince me that perhaps after all I had not been drowned.

My father thoroughly enjoyed his two-week August vacation at the Vineyard farmhouse, and so did we. Besides doing a great deal of reading he spent much time with the boys hiking over the countryside and taking them out fishing with some of the Vineyard fishermen. There were sumptuous meals in the homes of old friends, and we had many days together at the beach, traveling there and back in the borrowed farm-wagon.

Father did not often reprimand the boys and hardly ever the girls, but when he did, it was remembered. Twice while he was with us at the Vineyard he came down hard. Once it was because of a homemade merry-go-round the boys had painstakingly put together following directions in *The Youths' Companion*. To the top of a pole so tall and heavy they could hardly lift it they attached at right angles a shorter pole, and from each end of this they suspended a rope swing. They planted this contraption in a deep hole they dug, then persuaded my sister and me to climb into the swings. By running and pulling long ropes fastened to the crosspieces the boys turned the swings around at some speed, giving Helen and me a wild ride many feet above the ground. We yelled a lot, but really found it enjoyably exhilarating.

The boys could hardly wait for their father's arrival to show him this remarkable merry-go-round in action. To their dismay, when he saw Helen and me swinging wildly nearly straight out from the center pole, he did not applaud. Instead, he shouted, "Stop it! Take that thing down! Do you want to kill your sisters?" And he ran for an ax and began himself to cut down the poles and chop them into firewood. The boys were dumbfounded. What a bitter disappointment! They had been so proud of their splendid achievement and now, after all those hours of backbreaking work, their masterpiece was gone forever. "Never, never do a thing like that again," Father commanded. And the fact that they had found their instructions in the respected *Youths' Companion* did not save them from one of the worst tongue-lashings they ever had.

The other punishment fell on only one of the boys—the eldest. Many sheep grazed on the rolling Vineyard pastures, and on one of their walks of exploration the boys discovered a small slaughter-house. The gory scene, orchestrated with the sheeps' plaintive *baas* and made vivid by severed sheeps' heads lying about, drew the boys like a magnet and, unknown to their parents, they returned often.

One day, urged on by some inner demon, Walter decided it would be fun to give his little sister a scare. He promised me that if I would come on a long walk with him he would show me something exciting—but it must be kept a secret between us. Flattered by this unusual attention from my big brother I walked across the fields with him and saw the bloody scene. The result was more than Walter expected. I broke away from him, vomited, and ran all the way home, crying. But I did not forget my promise not to tell, and it was only my repeated nightmares that brought the matter to light. Without hesitation Father took the guilty boy to the barn for a thrashing that made his backside sore for a week. As for me, it was many years before I could abide the taste of lamb.

When the yellow blossoms on the long rows of potatoes on neighboring farms indicated that the potatoes in the ground below were nearly ripe, the boys decided to earn a little money by working for a nearby farmer digging them. It would be easy, they thought, but a day of stooping, digging, picking up and dumping potatoes into sacks showed them differently. Walter and Rob gave up at the end of the first day, but Herbert returned the next morning because, although he was no less stiff than the others, he had bargained with the farmer for a day's use of a horse in exchange for a day of potato-digging.

A few days later Herbert returned to the farm for the reward his heart was set on—a day of carefree horseback riding. One of the farmer's sons helped him mount the broad-backed horse from a stone wall and, sitting proudly erect on his blanket saddle, Herbert rode down the farm lane. All morning he guided the old horse up and down country roads. By noon he was ready for dinner, and he turned the horse toward home. He was not sitting quite so straight now, and there were aches in unaccustomed places, but he was still determined to have his full day's ride. He rode all afternoon; then, toward the end of the day, he turned into the lane leading to the barn where the horse belonged. He was bent nearly double. Like his young rider, the horse too had had enough. With a sudden motion he threw his inexperienced rider over his head and galloped up the lane to a well-earned rest in his stall. Unhurt, though painfully sore, Herbert limped homeward. For a day he had been a horseman, but for a week he paid for the experience by using a cushion at his meals.

For five consecutive summers, three of them in the same commodious farmhouse and two more in one nearby, our family enjoyed healthful vacations on the Vineyard. Then came the move to a Connecticut town which was almost a resort in its own right, and it was no longer necessary to seek a summer-long refuge from city heat. And so, for every member of the parsonage family, the Vineyard vacations became a memory, happy and unforgettable.

4. Time to Move

In midwinter of my first full year in school my mother took Helen and me aside. "It's not certain yet," she told us, "and you mustn't breathe a word outside, but it's quite possible that in the spring we'll be moving."

The pastoral limit, a hallmark of Methodism for so long, had been lifted and many Methodist ministers were settling down for a stay much longer than the previous two-or-three-year term. Our father, however, believed that change was good for both church and pastor, and that a three-year pastorate was usually long enough. The church year ran from spring to spring, and in January, at the fourth quarterly conference of the official board of the church, the matter of a change of pastor was always discussed.

With the minister tactfully leaving the room, a vote was taken on whether to invite him to stay on for another year or to ask for a new man—unless earlier the minister had stated his desire to leave. But even when a charge was certain it would not be known who the church's new pastor would be, or where the present one would go, until the annual spring conference of all the churches of the area.

Meantime the presiding elder of the district (later called the district superintendent) would discuss with each of his ministers slated to move the various possibilities open. With the time limit gone and preachers staying longer in the same place, there were fewer openings. Moves might become as complicated as in a game of chess, but under the Methodist system, with the assignment of churches, no minister need worry about being without a parish and no church about being without a pastor.

Once the decision for a change was announced, speculation about the next home became the leading topic of conversation in the parsonage. Our parents did not tell us the possibilities they and the presiding elder discussed privately, believing it was better not to mention uncertainties. No matter how we teased them to tell us where the "P.E." had said we might go, we got nowhere. Mother would, however, sound us out on preferences. Did we enjoy living in a city or might we find it interesting to live in a smaller place? How would we like to live near the water again?

We were reasonably sure that our new home would not be in a real country place although we knew our father, having grown up on a farm and enjoying rural things, would have liked this. Mother, we knew, preferred a town or city where, she said, schools and cultural opportunities were better. My brothers said this was because she had grown up in a small city, but we knew that Father would concede to her as he usually did. He believed that the Lord's work waited to be done everywhere; he would do his best to be a good minister of the gospel in whatever part of the Father's Vineyard he was sent to serve.

On a study shelf stood a thick book containing descriptive and historical sketches of all the Methodist parishes in "our" Conference—the New England Southern. It was illustrated with many photographs of ministers and their wives, leading laymen, churches, and parsonages. For hours at a stretch my sister and I pored over the pages of this big book. The historical sections left us cold, but we looked intently at every picture of a parsonage and discussed them all—this one seemed larger than our present home; that one had a porch; another appeared to have a big yard.

On a late winter Saturday morning, following breakfast and prayers, dishes and beds, Mother might invite Helen and me to go up attic with her before doing the usual Saturday-morning chores. We needed no second invitation. We stood by, all eyes, as she took clothing out of large wooden boxes and trunks, shook each article to make sure that no moths had found their way into the woolens despite mothballs, and deliberated as to the future usefulness of each piece. The laces, fans, jet ornaments and such things, most of which she had brought from her New Jersey home, seemed too fancy for use in a minister's household. But my mother was a saver, and who knew when one of them might come in handy? In the end she carefully repacked nearly everything.

Getting ready to move was as stimulating to Mother as planning a campaign must be to a general. When whatever obviously held no possibility for future use was reluctantly discarded she began to check to see that all that remained was in good condition. Loose picture frames were glued, furniture legs tightened, upholstery mended, for the incoming family must inherit everything in as good condition, bar a little (very little) natural wear, as we had found it.

Besides church-owned furniture the family possessions included a parlor organ, a cherry chest, a wicker rocker and my little one, Father's bookcases, several good mattresses and pillows, many pictures, much china and glassware and incidental treasures. These personal possessions Mother insisted contributed enough to our comfort and pleasure to compensate for the work they added at moving time. Then the organ had to be protected with blankets and quilts, the chest drawers packed with light articles, pillows tied around furniture legs, towels around big pictures, and old newspapers padded about each piece of china and glass before it was packed in a barrel.

The church authorities must have thought a spring moving date best for the churches and for the ministers. The busy winter program was then winding down and the lighter work of summer would give the new minister and the church a period of adjustment before the faster tempo of autumn set in. But for the members of the minister's family who were attending school a spring move was certainly not too good. It meant going into a new class and getting used to a different teacher, different courses, different books, all when the school year was nearing a close. But we parsonage children were too excited with the prospect of a new home and new adventures to worry much about school problems ahead of time.

We were enjoying too the pleasant things that went on in the church we were leaving. At meetings of the various organizations the minister's wife was often presented with a going-away gift, such as a small picture, a silver card tray, or a cut-glass bonbon dish. Children of church members gave small parties for Helen and me, and there were dinner or supper invitations for the whole family. Although my mother graciously accepted these invitations and appreciated their friendliness she confessed that sometimes it was more work to see that every member of the family was ready and properly dressed for a meal in someone else's house than to prepare a simple one at home.

As moving day drew near the tempo of daily life increased. Piles of old newspapers grew in cellar and back hall. Part of a lesser-used ground-floor room, usually the parlor, was cleared by transferring everything movable from it to some other room, laying papers over the freed area to protect the carpet, and bringing up a few empty wooden boxes and barrels from the cellar or woodshed where they had been stored.

My mother prided herself on being an expert packer. Helen and I helped her scour every room for objects which the family could get along without for a while; these we piled up near the empty containers. Then Mother would seat herself before a box or barrel, carefully line it with newspapers, then direct Helen or me to bring her first some flat, heavy things. These formed the bottom layer; after them came irregularly shaped things surrounded with soft articles. Mother's fingers would deftly explore the partly packed container for cavities. "Find me something square," she would say. Or "Bring me something round." Or, looking about and pointing, "That looks as if it would fit here." She seemed to use the same sort of skill and get the same kind of pleasure that many people do from fitting together pieces of a jigsaw puzzle. When it came to clothing, she followed the "smooth and flat" school, preferring very long boxes for coats and dresses so she could put them in full length.

After the last cranny in a box was filled and the contents level with the top, Mother would test her work with a gentle pressure of her hands, fill any tiny crevice with an equally tiny article and, when the surface was almost as even as a tabletop, would cover it with newspapers folded lengthwise. On the side of the box she would print a number which she also entered in a notebook together with a brief description of the box's contents. "Now," she would say contentedly, "we'll know where we're at when we unpack." For already her mind was running ahead to the day of unpacking and the desirability of opening boxes according to the family's need. In general this would mean opening first the boxes with the highest numbers—those that were packed last and so contained essentials such as kitchen utensils and tableware.

After my mother had finished packing several boxes and barrels it was my father's turn. He and the boys carried the heavy containers to the woodshed or some other more or less out-of-the-way place for the covers to be put on. Now the sound of the hammer was heard in the house, and my father's demand for nails, and still more nails.

Father was not so deft with his hands as many men, and certainly not so fast. Yet I think he rather enjoyed deliberately measuring and fitting boards together for box and barrel covers, sawing them to the right length, and nailing them down. I think he liked too, as I did, the smell of the new lumber he had bought. The whole manual task, I believe, gave him real pleasure and a sense of accomplishment. Perhaps, since his lifework dealt with imponderables and immeasurables he found it relaxing to do something where the results were highly visible.

When he finished putting on a cover Father would give the last nail a final whack or two, take the half dozen nails from between his lips, and straighten up. Surveying the finished boxes and then the four or five more waiting for him to cover he would mutter gloomily, "Don't know why on earth your mother wants so much stuff." Then, giving a hitch to his suspenders and a turn to his rolled-up shirtsleeves he would begin to measure boards for the next box or barrel.

But when it came to packing his library the shoe was on the other foot. "I'm sure you don't need all those books," my mother would protest. "Why don't you pass a few of them on to some new preacher?"

"You never know when you'll need a book," my father would reply. "I wouldn't give up one of them."

Book-packing was left entirely in his hands. It was a lengthy process, for he could not resist stealing a look here and reading a paragraph or two there. His first move was to set aside the books he thought he might need in the next few weeks. The others he directed Helen and me to arrange in piles according to size after slapping them together to get out the dust, then wiping the edges with a rag. Later I resented this method, but the books seemed to survive it. He packed the small piles we handed him into extra heavy wooden boxes, wedging wadded newspapers wherever there was a gap. So skillfully did he pack that there was rarely a marred cover or edge. Father did not begrudge the time or effort spent in book-packing, for his library was his delight as well as an essential tool in his work.

Reinforced boxes were used for books, but barrels were used for sermons. Each sermon was written longhand on half sheets, often with additional notes scribbled on scrap paper—backs of old letters, even long envelopes slit to give considerable writing surface—then filed in a manila envelope. On this Father carefully wrote theme and text, followed by place and date of delivery. This list might be quite lengthy, as the same sermon, being new to each different audience, could be used many times. That, Father used to say laughingly, was one of the advantages of frequent moves. Packing sermons in barrels was an accepted ministerial custom, and the inspiration of quips often heard among Methodist preachers. "Scraping the bottom of the barrel" described a poor sermon. "Time to turn the barrel" could mean that a move to another place was advisable.

By the time Father left to attend the Annual Conference much of the packing was done. Of course there was the off chance that some slip might occur and the bishop presiding at the Conference might overrule the presiding elder's recommendation and return the minister to his old parish. Fortunately this rarely occurred. But during Conference week the deliberations between the bishop and the three presiding elders in charge of the three Conference districts might, and often did, result in last-minute switches which changed well-laid plans and sometimes gave a minister a pastorate he had not anticipated. Not until the list of appointments was read from the podium on the last day of the

Conference could any minister be absolutely sure where his next year's assignment would be. And with long-distance communication being costly and not too commonly used, it was generally not until he returned to his home that his family shared his knowledge.

So far as I know no unexpected move was ever our lot. Everything went as Father and Mother had thought probable, but now it was official and the children learned where their new home would be. Father would tell us pleasant things he had heard about the place, and Mother would ask him questions calculated to bring answers to whet our enthusiasm. "I'm told it's a nice church," he would say; "the people are friendly, and yes, the parsonage is roomy."

Now we were ready for the final lap of the packing ordeal. As soon as all boxes and barrels were filled it was time to begin on trunks and suitcases. Half a dozen old trunks, two or three "extension bags" (which were truly that), several straw and leather suitcases were packed with personal belongings. Trunks were filled until they had to be sat on to be closed—and loud wails went up as fingers got caught in the process.

On one occasion at this stage the mailman brought a card from the minister who was to take Father's place. It stated the day on which the movers would arrive with his family's belongings. "But they can't," Mother protested. "That's the day *our* movers are coming to take ours out!"

"We must adjust," Father said firmly. "They have made their plans just as we have made ours."

My mother bit her lip and for a while was glumly silent. Then her face brightened. "I see now how it can be managed," she said. "Our movers can use the back door and theirs the front one. That way our things can be going out at the back while theirs are coming in at the front and the two sets of things won't get mixed." And so it was done, although fortunately the two teams of movers did not overlap by much.

The last days before departure from the old home were hectic ones. Many people called to say goodby, often bringing with them some little token for remembrance or some hearty dish or tasty dessert for us to enjoy. Meals were sketchy affairs eaten picnic style at the kitchen table. Everyone seemed in a hurry all the time.

My anticipation of the new place began to be mingled with

43

regrets at leaving the old one. I bade my school friends a teary farewell, doubtful now that I would ever again have such good companions. Our last Sunday was full of sober farewells and more cheerful good wishes, highlighted by a lavish Sunday dinner in a parishioner's home. All of us were beginning to realize that a time of change was both sad and happy, and that, being a Methodist minister's family, this was a fact of life we might as well accept and learn to live with.

II
The Middle Years

5. As a Family

With the move to Connecticut when I was almost seven it was conceded that I was no longer "the baby" but a responsible member of the family group. "Remember," Father told us soon after arriving in the new home, "we stand together as a family. If any one of you gets into trouble it reflects on us all and on the church too. As minister's children you are expected to set a good example. Choose your friends carefully and always try to do what is right. Another thing—remember that what goes on in the parsonage is no one else's affair. Some people have an oversized bump of curiosity and they will try to pump the minister's children to find out things that are none of their business. Edith, you're old enough now to understand this. Be polite, but keep quiet and act dumb if you have to when people ask you questions about what goes on in the parsonage."

His warning to me was not unnecessary, for often sweet-speaking ladies would try to extract from the youngest member of the family what they had not been able to pry out of its older members. "That was Mr. Smith at your house for dinner yesterday, wasn't it?" . . . "I notice your father's been calling on old Mrs. Green almost every day. Does he think she's failing?" . . . "Has young Jones come to see your father about his wedding yet?"

Nothing resembling the modern church office existed on the church premises, and the pastor's parsonage study was where much of the business of the church was conducted. No matter how small the house, one room must always be set aside for the minister to receive his callers, administer his parish, answer his correspondence (in longhand), prepare his sermons, and study his Bible. It was also the place where, I am certain, our minister father prayed often and devoutly to his God.

In a large and lively household it was difficult to keep this room as quiet and removed from the current of daily life as would have been desirable. We all tried—when we remembered—to do this. The unavoidable sounds connected with the comings and goings of an active family did not seem to bother my father too much, or if they did, he did not often complain. Only on Saturdays and early Sundays would Mother remind us to be really quiet because "Father is working on his sermon."

Mealtimes were very much family affairs. On schooldays the noon meal was necessarily hurried in spite of its being the hearty one of the day. Suppers were more leisurely, sometimes even gay. Around the big table, after the usual brief blessing, we were treated to the day's news, the funny things that had happened in school, rumors of newcomers to the town, plans for coming activities. We were encouraged to air our opinions on almost any subject. Conversation was lively and non-stop.

Walter: Old Man Jones has a new ear trumpet. Did you know that, Father?

Father: Mr. Jones, Walter. Yes, I know, and I hope it works, though I haven't much faith in such contrivances.

Helen: Mr. Jones may have a new trumpet, but *Mrs.* Jones has a new hat. It was in Sharples' window all week with a $4.50 price tag on it.

Mother: That's an unnecessary comment, Helen. Edith, you forgot to bring the butter up from the cellar. Please go down and get it.

Edith: Everyone makes me run errands just because I'm the youngest.

Walter: Let's hope you always are.

Father: That's enough of such talk, Walter.

Interruptions were frequent. When several children tried to talk at the same time—or with food in the mouth—Mother would intervene and add a little lecture on the importance of good table manners. "You must learn to eat like ladies and gentlemen," she would say, and she would murmur such admonitions as "Elbows off the table," "Use your knife," or "Unfold your napkin."

When callers came near mealtime it was considered only natural to invite them to stay and share our noonday dinner or evening supper. Then we were expected to talk less and listen more— which we did with good grace when, as frequently happened, the guest talked intelligently and perhaps even told amusing stories.

Often when we were by ourselves at supper we would tell jokes or propound original riddles. Or we might play a guessing game, or make someone give a three-minute speech on a certain subject. These "fun" suppers were also a kind of "royal road to learning," for Father insisted that any question of grammar, spelling, or meaning must be cleared up immediately and authoritatively. As the youngest, I was the one most often sent to bring from the study the appropriate volume of *The Century Dictionary and Cyclopedia.* Knowing the alphabet order was important for if I took the wrong volume I would have to trot back for the right one.

Family disagreements were not to be brought up at mealtimes. Mother or Father settled petty quarrels among the children privately, and never did one parent override the decision of the other. "Whatever your mother says goes," was Father's decisive statement. And when Mother said, "Ask your father," we knew there would be no recourse from his verdict.

Approaching seventeen, Walter began to feel infinitely wiser than his fourteen- and fifteen-year-old brothers and to crave greater independence. His interest had been captured by the small printing press the boys had worked on together and, finishing high school, he elected to learn the printing business. He became a

"printer's devil" in a small printing office in nearby New London
—the first stage in what proved to be a long and successful career.
His working hours and his widening interests meant that activities
undertaken as a family now often had to get along without Walter.
By making the front part of the attic into a tiny bedroom he
achieved a room of his own, and out of his meager weekly wages
he subscribed to a printing journal. He also paid his parents a small
amount for room and board, but he was not allowed to forget that
he was still a member of the family and bound by its responsibilities. Our parents, we noticed, instead of talking about "the boys,"
now almost always spoke of "Walter and the boys." Herbert and
Rob, both planning to go on to college, were continuing with
their studies in a New London preparatory school.

To promote family solidarity, more activities involving us all
were planned. A croquet set was planted in the wide lawn and
we all, Father and Mother included, became expert at the sport of
whacking balls through wickets. Tossing beanbags through the
different-sized holes of a wooden board set up on the lawn was
another family diversion, and at the far end of the yard two
iron stakes were hammered into the ground for pitching horseshoes. A pile of these, which were easy to come by in this era
when automobiles were a novelty and horse-drawn vehicles the
usual means of transportation, was placed just inside the woodshed
door. Sometimes when Father heard the sharp click of the iron
shoes he would suddenly appear to join the game Herbert and Rob
were having. "Been cooped up in the study too long to think
straight," he would say. "Need to clear my brain." But with his
strong belief in a well-balanced life—spiritual, mental, physical—
he had no need to apologize.

Helen's and my amusements were tamer. When in midsummer a
nearby hilltop meadow was white with daisies we liked to go there
to pick them to carry to one of the church shut-ins. Sometimes
we would take a snack of bread and jelly and a banana and midway in our picking would climb a great rock which stood in the
middle of the meadow. There as we ate we would look at the distant river and wish we were on it.

In the cold months night fell early and evenings were long in
spite of early bedtime. After the study hour there were occasional
read-aloud sessions but oftener we read separately or played
games. Mother was always ready to put down her reading or

sewing to join us in a game of dominoes, parcheesi, halma, authors, or anagrams. Father's favorite game was checkers. Once or twice during the winter months Herbert would work out a complicated schedule for a family checker tournament. I was always the first to drop out, then Helen. Winners were pitted against winners until the finalists, usually Father and Herbert, played the last match.

When young people came in for the evening we often played a lively game called "Donkey." This was a sort of substitute game for playing cards, which were considered a "device of the devil" and were never seen in our home. Played with cards cut from colored cardboard and bearing different numbers, Donkey seemed to satisfy the players unacquainted with regular playing cards.

One Christmas brought the gift of a carom board—a polished wood, yard-square parlor version of a billiard table. Rather surprisingly this was not frowned on as a possible introduction to the "low-down" pool parlor. Instead, it was enjoyed by the whole family, especially Walter and the boys and their young friends.

Music played a large part in our family life. Even before high-school days each of the boys had earned enough money to pay a good share of the cost of a musical instrument, the balance coming from Mother's stringent budgeting. Soon the household was richer—and noisier—by the addition of a violin, a clarinet, and a cornet. Practice, however, had to be limited to hours when Father was not in his study—unless the beginning musician wished to use the cellar or the woodshed as a studio.

Helen had early shown such talent at playing the little reed parlor organ that the Brockton church organist had insisted on giving her free music lessons. By the time she was twelve or so the little old organ was so obviously inadequate that my mother decided it must be replaced by a piano. The boys protested that this was unfair and that Helen was being favored over them. Why, the cost of the piano would be more than that of their three instruments combined! Artfully Mother projected the idea of a family orchestra with Helen at the piano, Walter playing the violin, Herbert the clarinet, and Rob the cornet. "And what about me?" I wailed. "You can stand beside the piano and turn the pages when Helen nods," I was told. All were appeased, and the acquisition of a piano became a family matter of prime importance.

From a nest egg more or less secretly stowed away for a rainy day Mother produced the—to us—astronomical amount required to buy a good upright piano. Taking with her a member of the church whose musical judgment she trusted, she went to Hartford where they toured the music stores and departments and returned with the promise of the early delivery of a piano. It was a big day for us when the delivery van rolled up and the piano was brought in to replace the organ in our parlor. Helen could hardly be dragged away from it long enough to eat. It gave impetus to the boys' progress with their musical instruments, and after many evenings of practice the projected family orchestra became a reality. It even became good enough to be invited to play at friends' homes and at informal church affairs. My turning of pages being oftener too early or too late, however, I was kindly requested to become one of the audience.

With the arrival of summer, family diversions turned to outside activities. The river ran by the end of our street only a couple of blocks away, so it was natural that my brothers became enamored with things along the waterfront. They haunted the wharves, went fishing from the ends of them and out boating as often as they were invited. Soon they became obsessed with the idea of owning a boat themselves. Since a sailboat was obviously a luxury far beyond their accumulated savings they realized they would have to be content with a smaller craft. To Mother, with her dread of water, any kind of boat spelled probable disaster, but Father rather encouraged the boys in their ambition. Rowing, he told Mother, was good exercise, and a boat might be something the whole family could enjoy. Mother finally conceded that if there must be a boat a rowboat would probably be the least dangerous.

So the boys and their father went shopping along the riverfront and eventually, with their combined resources, acquired a sturdy flat-bottomed rowboat, large enough, Father said, to hold the whole family. For awhile Herbert and Rob became regular river rats, showing up only for meals and slighting their chores and small paid jobs. It took a lecture from Father and blisters from rowing to bring their enthusiasm under control.

Now began our family midweek summer picnics. Only Walter, working faithfully at his job, was missing as one by one, loaded to the chin, we straggled down the street to the big rowboat. One lugged two pairs of oars, another the big picnic basket, while others carried bathing suits, towels, wraps, books, and Mother's sewing bag.

Once, halfway down the street, we passed a schoolmate of mine standing at his gate. As each of us went by he turned and shouted back toward an open window, "Here comes another Patterson, Maw. . . . Maw, here comes *another* Patterson." For years my mother used these words to shame us out of stringing along tandem fashion when we were bound as a family for church or elsewhere.

When all of us and our equipment were finally loaded into the boat Father and the boys pushed it away from the wharf, the two sets of oars were put into motion, and the boat moved slowly against the tide or more swiftly with it up or down the broad river.

A favorite picnic spot upstream was a grove above a steep bluff a mile or two away on the other side of the river. Or we might go farther, to a flat tree-shaded place just before the uninteresting stretch of marshland began. Going downstream we passed under two bridges, passenger and rail, and continued on to a sizable island which at that time was an almost deserted area of rocks and trees. Here, after the boat was unloaded and dragged up on the sand, we would set up our headquarters on a large sloping rock shaded by leafy trees, then, having changed into our cover-up bathing suits behind bushes, would head for the water. While Father and the boys swam, Mother and Helen and I would wade and splash about. No attempt was made to teach my sister and me to swim, for swimming Mother did not consider a suitable sport for girls. Later, over a fire built from wood we gathered easily, Mother heated the stew, fried the meatballs, or warmed the hash she had brought for our hearty lunch. Each one buttered his own slices of homemade bread to eat with the fresh vegetables supplied from our own garden.

After lunch Father stretched out under a tree for his customary afternoon nap, then did a bit of reading in the book he was sure to have brought along. The boys went rowing or fishing or played ball on the shore. Mother very likely propped herself against a tree and did some sewing, and Helen and I gathered pebbles on the beach or wandered inland to pick wild flowers. It was a light-hearted, relaxing day for everyone. Toward dusk we piled into the boat for the row home. If the tide had turned against us while we had been ashore our homeward progress would be slower, and sometimes, in spite of the lengthy summer days, it was almost dark when we took our loads, with only the big picnic basket lighter, up the street to home.

These pleasant river excursions so dulled my mother's fear of water that the second summer she listened to the boys' pleas to add a sail to the rowboat. It must, she insisted, be the smallest size that was practicable, and with Father's help such a sail was purchased. Its addition delighted the boys and the rest of us, with the possible exception of Mother.

Yet she relented enough when still another boating season arrived to allow the boys to increase the size of the sail—but by no more than one foot all around. If they would agree to this stipulation she promised to help them buy the canvas and to stitch it onto the old sail. This proved to be a more difficult task than she anticipated, but she persisted until it was done—and well done, thanks to her skill and her trusty sewing machine.

Now the little boat became easily identifiable on the river even at some distance, for while the main part of the sail was yellowed from the year of exposure the foot-wide strip around it was pristinely white. But who cared! The boat sailed better, and even Walter, who more and more was going out on bigger boats with older friends, condescended to sail in it on some of his free days or half days. Never, of course, on Sunday.

It was a humble boat, as boats go—that rowboat transformed into a sailboat—but it was one in which we all took pride. It was a major family possession which we treasured as highly in summer as we did the upright piano in winter.

6. The Seemly Sabbath

Sunday in our parsonage home was in every way the First Day of the Week, the Lord's Day, the Sabbath. Other families might think of the week as being made up of six days and Sunday; for us it consisted of Sunday with the other days leading up to it.

Serious preparations for the Sabbath began early on Saturday. That morning the downstairs rooms were cleaned. Quietly though, so that Father, at work on his sermon in the study above, would not be disturbed. The carpet sweeper propelled by Mother was nearly noiseless and so were the dustcloths reluctantly wielded by Helen and me. My task was to wipe the more or less indestructible legs of tables and chairs. Helen was entrusted with the more delicate job of polishing tabletops and dusting the possibly fragile objects on them.

To her also fell the disagreeable job of the weekly care and filling of lamps. Every Saturday morning I helped her gather them from every room and place them on a thick pad of newspapers spread on the kitchen table. There she cleaned and polished the china, glass, or metal outsides, trimmed the wicks so that the flame would burn evenly, and filled the lamps from the spout of the two-quart kerosene can brought up from the cellar. Transferring operations to the sink, she wiped off with old newspapers any soot which might have accumulated on the chimneys, then washed them in sudsy warm water, followed by a hot-water rinse and careful drying.

As soon as the lamp work was finished, Mother began to hover over the big black coal or wood-burning kitchen range. Cooking was heavy on Saturday so that it could be held to a minimum on Sunday. Beans which had been put to soak Friday night boiled slowly most of Saturday morning. Mother used "yellow-eyed" beans in preference to the small white navy beans many housewives favored, with a few dried lima beans added to them for flavor. Before putting the boiled beans in a beanpot she salted them, and added a generous flavoring of molasses, a dash of mustard, and a hunk of salt pork. All Saturday afternoon they baked slowly, with water added from time to time to make them moist and tender. Toward the end of the afternoon the pot was uncovered so that the top beans, with the hunk of salt pork jutting up, would become delectably crusty and crisp when, conforming to the New England custom, we ate them, along with brown bread and piccalilli, for Saturday-night supper.

Besides the beans on Saturday morning the front of the stove was taken up with a large pot roast of beef—our usual weekend meat. This was served hot for Saturday noon dinner and cold for Sunday dinner. Cabbage and potatoes went with it on Saturday and warmed-over baked beans and potatoes on Sunday.

All day Saturday the tank in the back of the stove was kept full of water heating for the traditional Saturday-night baths. As soon as the water in the tank became hot it was dipped out with the useful long-handled dipper and poured into the copper washboiler which had been brought up from the cellar and set on the stove above the tank, and the tank refilled with water from the faucet. There could never be too much hot water for bath night!

No outside activities were permitted for Saturday evening. After our bean supper Father went to his study to work on his sermon and Helen and I stripped the dining-room table—there would be clean linen on Sunday. The table became covered with Bibles, Sunday-school lesson leaflets, and Peloubet's Sunday-school notes, for this was the hour for studying our Sunday-school lessons. No talk was allowed as we gathered around the table, except an occasional whispered question to Mother who, as a Sunday-school teacher, had her lesson to study too. The only sound was the creaking of the overhead hanging lamp as it was adjusted to suit individual preferences, now up, now down, and never, naturally, without some whispered argument.

After half an hour or so Helen and I were excused and sent upstairs to disrobe in our chilly bedroom, wrap ourselves in flannel dressing gowns, and patter down to the superheated kitchen. In the center stood two wooden tubs which the boys had brought up from the cellar. Mother poured a scanty supply of the precious hot water into them and tempered it with water from the tap. Two kettles hummed cheerfully on the front of the stove to augment the hot-water supply in tank and boiler.

"Hurry up out there," the brothers called, "it's our turn!" Helen and I paid little attention, knowing that their impatience stemmed less from a desire for cleanliness than from wanting release from the enforced Bible study.

Saturday-night sleep was sound, and morning came soon. But there was no luxurious lingering in bed for the minister's household. We were up and at breakfast in good time, enjoying the change from our usual hot cereal to our "Sunday-morning special" of omelet and toast. *"Sh-sh,"* Mother warned if we spoke too loudly. "Don't disturb your father's thinking."

After-breakfast prayers were briefer on Sunday. Instead of the usual Scripture reading by Father we recited together a psalm—perhaps the hundredth, or the first, or the twenty-third. These were joined in without hesitation by everyone, for they had been learned almost as early as the A-B-C's. This unison recital took less time, which was especially precious on Sabbath mornings, and it saved Father's voice for the heavy demands of the day. After the prayer—shorter than on week days—Father hurried back to the study to spend a final hour on his sermon while the rest of us did the essential household chores and then got ourselves dressed for this important weekly appearance.

Occasionally raised voices must have penetrated the study walls. "Ma, I can't find my good petticoat." . . . "Who stole my blue tie?" . . . "Where's my white shirt?" . . . "I just stuck my toe through my stocking."

Mother was everywhere. "Herbert, your shoes need shining. You should have attended to that yesterday." . . . "Walter, there's a button missing on your coat. Bring it here quickly. I'll try to find another button and sew it on. I know it's not right to do it on the Sabbath, but I guess the Lord will forgive me this once." . . . "Helen, brush your hair more carefully." All this while managing to get herself suitably attired to meet the critical gaze of a hundred pairs of eyes.

When the church bell began to peal Mother would cast an appraising glance over each of us, missing no stocking hole, soiled collar, dirty earlobe, or look of uncombed hair and seeing that the fault was speedily corrected. Father would emerge from the study, give his thick hair a hurried last-minute brush, button on his stiffly starched collar and bow tie, and don his ministerial-looking Prince Albert frock coat. Setting his derby decorously on his head he would leave by the front door, walking as speedily as Sunday-morning decorum would permit.

The minister's family soon followed in a straggly sort of procession. A skip on the part of the youngest brought a stern reproof: "Daughter, walk, do not skip. Remember this is the Sabbath Day and you are on your way to the House of God." To Helen: "Do try to stand up straighter. Mrs. Jones is just behind, watching every one of us." And to Herbert, surreptitiously trying to clean his nails as he walked along: "Stop that at once! That is as unseemly a thing to do in public as to brush your teeth." Pocketing his nailfile we could hear Herbert mutter, "But a lot more convenient."

Smiles, bows, and polite how-do-you-do's greeted us as we approached the church, mounted the steps, and entered the vestibule. Then came the hateful walk down the aisle to the minister's pew, third or fourth from the front, with all of us acutely aware of the eyes upon us. In the pew Mother put one daughter on either side of her, while her sons took their places at the end of the pew.

As the youngest, my squirmings during the service were tolerated though discouraged. I liked best the standing-up parts, especially the congregational hymn-singing. It was hard not to turn and stare at a woman whose loud, slightly off-key singing I knew annoyed my father, but I had been warned against doing this and resolutely kept my eyes ahead. Next to the singing I enjoyed most the collection-taking, with the ushers passing the big silver plates to the people in the pews. As early as I began having pennies of my own I had been taught to put some of them aside in a small envelope as a thank-offering to God. When the usher reached our pew I myself placed the envelope in the plate, even before my mother and sister and brothers put in theirs.

Almost across the aisle from us sat a dozen or so boys and girls accompanied by two women. The children were well behaved, but even the first time I saw them I realized that there was something out of the ordinary about them. Their eyes were restless and seemed to be taking in everything around them. And so they were, and so they had to do, for, as I soon learned, these children were deaf mutes, boarding pupils at a nearby special school for boys and girls handicapped in this way. At first I was startled by the squeaky little squeals with which they greeted us when we shook hands with them after the service, but after a time this no longer bothered me.

A deep feeling of pride swept over me as I looked up at my father standing behind the pulpit so erect and, I thought, handsome. I listened entranced as he read from the Bible or recited, as he often did, the first verse of the hymn the congregation was about to sing. No matter if I did not exactly understand all the words, such lines as "The spacious firmament on high" filled me with pleasure. So did the music of the psalms, the stern voices of the prophets, the comforting words of Jesus. Somehow my father's voice conveyed to me the mysticism, the power and the glory, the divine compassion and the human compulsion in the words. His Scripture reading was often really recitation, with only an occasional glance at the Bible opened before him, for much of the King James Version was as familiar to him as "Now I lay me" was to me. No one in his congregation, I am sure, could doubt that to their minister the Bible was God's Word, the absolute, incontrovertible truth, and his never-failing guide.

Father prided himself on preparing his forty-minute sermon so well that he did not need to read it or even to use notes. It seemed endlessly long to me except for the occasional stories, which he called illustrations. I waited impatiently for the moment toward the end when he would close the big Bible and take a step or two forward beside the pulpit. This was the "moment of truth," the time when he appealed to his listeners to accept more completely the Christ about whom he had been preaching. At this point his tone often held a note of pleading which brought a lump into my throat and made me fight back tears. To offset this I had to keep telling myself that this was the time I had been waiting for, the sign that the sermon was nearly over.

Once as Father stepped forward he knocked over a glass of water placed at the side of the pulpit. The glass fell to the floor, the water spilling out of it, and rolled unbroken down the two or three steps into the chancel. My father paused only long enough to glance down and remark, "No harm done, brethren." Thereafter when a slight mishap occurred at home this remark was often used.

One Sunday in midsummer Mother was kept home from church by a bad cold, and since I was not ready to go with my sister I was to follow by myself. Mother said I might carry the pink parasol I had been given on my birthday a short time earlier and which was my pride and joy. "Walk down the aisle slowly and quietly," she told me, "and sit between the boys and Helen."

Proudly holding the parasol above me I walked the short distance to the church and climbed the steps. I entered the sanctuary and walked down the center aisle—slowly and quietly, as Mother had said—still holding the pink parasol above me. I kept my eyes straight ahead, though I had a feeling that people were looking at me and smiling. As I reached the family pew an usher stooped over and gently closed my parasol. This, I assumed, was something he did for every lady who carried a parasol to church, and I smiled my thanks. Why my brothers were giggling softly as I squeezed past them or why Helen scowled at me I did not understand. After church Helen told me sharply that no one ever carried an open parasol indoors, especially in church. But at home my mother did not scold me and Father laughed and said it was something he had never before seen in church.

Each Sunday, when the concluding hymn had been sung and the benediction pronounced, the people in the congregation quietly greeted one another and shook hands with their minister, who had a friendly word and a warm handclasp for each of them. The children hurried on into the Sunday-school room where Sunday school started with a brief period of lively songs and exercises before breaking up into separate class groups. Because of the previous evening's study the minister's children were well prepared for the week's lesson.

Sunday school over, we rushed for home. We were hungry for dinner but we knew we had to wait for the flame to be set to the fire already laid in the kitchen range, for the water to heat and the potatoes to be boiled, the Saturday-night beans to be warmed up, and the pot roast sliced. The boy or girl whose weekly duty it was to put on the table the four essentials—"bread, butter, water, milk" —must do his or her job (and later bring out from the pantry the cold tapioca or rice or cornstarch pudding for dessert). Father was rarely home for Sunday dinner; while we were in Sunday school he left to go to a neighboring village to preach in his second church. Often, however, we had a guest with us.

One Sunday Mother invited a young man to have dinner with us. He disappeared for a few moments after Sunday school and when he reappeared he was carrying a carton of ice cream. It was a tense moment, for all of us had been taught that it was wicked to buy anything on the Sabbath. We wondered what Mother would do. We saw her hesitate as the young man presented the package to her, then we sighed with relief as she accepted it graciously. "We do not make a practice of patronizing shopkeepers who break the Sabbath by remaining open on the Lord's Day," Mother told him (knowing that we were listening), "but we do appreciate your thoughtfulness and we shall all enjoy the ice cream." As an afterthought she added, "No doubt it was *made* yesterday."

After the Sunday dinner dishes were done we could spend the afternoon according to our individual preferences—except that most of them were considered unseemly on the Sabbath. Music was limited to hymns. Loud talking and "worldly" conversation were out of order, as were games, needlework, or carpentry, even whittling. One exception to the no-games rule was the solving of the "enigma" printed each week in the Sunday-school paper. Since it was based on a Bible verse this was allowed—also, the boys suggested, because Mother was so fond of puzzles.

Sunday reading must be confined to the Bible, devotional or inspirational books, tracts, church or Sunday-school papers, or a few Christmas-gift books with anemic pictures and moralistic stories. One startling book brought out on Sundays was an oversized edition of Dante's *Inferno* with the famous Gustav Doré illustrations.

These horrifying pictures were, I am sure, responsible for many nightmares of my childhood. Needless to say no Sunday newspapers ever crossed our threshold; we were even forbidden to read borrowed copies later in the week. Knowing no better, we believed they were filled with unreliable news items, social scandals, and reports of prize fights and other immoral events. In addition, they encouraged Sabbath-breaking on the part of their distributors, vendors, and newsboys.

Letter-writing on Sunday afternoons was permissible. So was taking a long walk—quietly and with decorum as befitted the Lord's Day. Or one might take a nap. In some parishes during winter months there was an hour-long meeting of the Junior League at the church on Sunday afternoons and this Helen and I were expected to attend. Even with this interruption the clocks on Sunday afternoon seemed always to tick more slowly, as if conspiring to prolong the dreary hours.

No regular meal was planned at night. Toward evening each of us would wander into the kitchen to get ourselves a "bite," perhaps a sandwich and an apple, or a dish of home-canned peaches or pears topped off with a piece of Mother's good "one-egg" sponge or spice cake.

At six-thirty everyone except Father, home now from his afternoon preaching service, went back to the church to attend the Epworth League meeting. Helen usually played the hymns, and Rob sometimes played along on his cornet. Although conducted by young people, older church people also came, most of them staying on for the evening service. This was less formal than the morning one. Instead of preaching a sermon Father usually gave a talk, often building it around some literary or historical figure. In spite of my end-of-a-long-day weariness I frequently became interested enough to ask him the next day to tell me more about that person.

The happiest part of the Sabbath for all of us, I believe, was the hour following our return from the evening service. Father was relaxed now and once again a family man after the long day devoted to his churches. We would join in a hymn-sing around the piano, with Helen playing. Then we would have something to eat together. It might be popcorn and apples, or cake and cocoa served in the best china cups, or in summer cookies and lemonade. And while we ate Father might relate an interesting anecdote of his childhood or college years, or he might recite from his rich store of poetry some lengthy narrative poem such as "The Cotter's Saturday Night."

The melodious rhythm of his voice and the flow of conversation often set me to head-nodding. Mother would rouse me, and in a stupor of sleep I would climb the stairs, undress, and, kneeling, mumble my prayers. As I tumbled into bed all the rigors and restraints of the Lord's Day in a minister's household would quite fade away and I would quickly fall asleep. Tomorrow would come soon, beginning a week full of activity and interest—one which would surely and certainly culminate in another seemly Sabbath.

7. Double Charge

The day of the circuit rider had disappeared before my time, but the "double charge" was still common in New England Methodism. A small church unable to support a minister of its own would often arrange to have the part-time services of a theological student, perhaps from Yale or Boston University, or of a pastor of a larger church in a neighboring town or city. This arrangement usually worked out well and was a great financial help to the student or minister, especially to one with a large family to feed and clothe.

Twice during my girlhood my father had a double charge. In both cases train or trolley connections between his main parish and the smaller one were poor or nonexistent. Since automobiles were far from commonplace and horse-drawn vehicles the customary means of conveyance, Father used a horse and buggy to get to his Sunday afternoon preaching service in his second charge. The turn-out provided by the local livery stable was always trim and tidy, and the horse neither a high stepper nor a sluggish plug. My father knew horses and enjoyed driving. In his journal he once wrote: "There is a contagion of life from a good horse," and again, "I would rather drive a horse full of life and that took some strength to guide than a slow, lazy one." Any horse he drove was well handled and well treated, and the livery-stable owner could be sure that one rented to "the parson" would be returned in good condition.

Usually Father drove alone to his Sunday afternoon service, but occasionally I was allowed to go with him. On those red-letter days I would tiptoe out of Sunday school at the end of the opening exercises, and while Father took a short nap I would get myself a hasty lunch. Joining me in the kitchen when it was about time for the livery-stable rig to arrive, he would beat up an egg with milk and drink it hurriedly.

The streets were almost deserted as we started out, and we would clip along at as lively a pace as my father thought seemly on the Sabbath. When we were well out of town Father would often, to my delight, hand me the reins, keeping the ends looped over his wrist. The horse, aware of the change of drivers, would slacken his pace, but by cluck-clucking to him I would urge him into a respectable trot. Father would pull his sermon notes from his pocket and begin to mull over the scribbled pieces of paper.

When once in a while we met one of the strange new horseless carriages Father would take the reins from me. By clucking reassuringly to the horse he somehow managed to diminish fear and convey confidence. If he had time and saw a car standing in front of a house he would stop, get out, and lead the horse up to and around the strange contraption, letting him sniff at it and look at as much of it as he could see from behind his confining blinders. I wondered whether this did any good and whether the horse would connect that stationary object with the fearful monster that came charging toward him on the road. I did not wonder at his fright— both the sound and the smell of those early cars were enough to panic more than a horse!

Once a rein broke when an automobile was approaching and my father was going through his reassuring clucking business. Startled, the horse twitched violently and started to run. With a quick lunge that almost plunged him over the dashboard Father succeeded in catching the other end of the broken rein. Still standing, he continued making comforting noises to the horse until he was able to calm and control the animal and bring him to a stop beside the road. "Thank God!" Father said devoutly as he got out. Using the hitching rope he fixed the rein temporarily and we went on. "Do you realize," he said to me, "that God delivered us from what might have been a very serious accident?"

As we approached the outskirts of the fishing village which was his second parish Father would put away his notes, pull out his big silver watch to see that we were on schedule, and take over the reins. At the church I was turned over to the "good ladies" while he went to an inner room to kneel in prayer before going into the pulpit. The ladies cooed and fussed over me until, as the little organ wheezed out a "piece," we all took our seats in the stiff pews.

Sitting through a second preaching service I accepted as the price to be paid for the pleasure of the ride. Frequently the sermon was the one I had heard at the home church in the morning. My attempts to anticipate the points were not very successful so I made a mental list of Things to Think About. Items on the list might include the fancy hat worn by a lady ahead of me, the movement of the leaves on the tree just outside the opened window, or the number of panes of glass in certain windows. Occasionally I passed the time by seeing how many things around me began with *A,* then with *B,* with *C,* and so on, but this gave me a guilty feeling. It was really a game, I told myself, and if playing games on Sunday was wrong, how much more wicked it must be to play them in church!

At last came the final hymn and the benediction, after which we stood around for what seemed to me a very long time as my father talked to different people. Sometimes we made several calls on sick and aged church members before we started home, and usually Father took me into the house with him. During the "word of prayer" (an understatement) with which each call ended I knelt beside my chair as I had been trained to do since babyhood. Sometimes instead of keeping my eyes closed I looked through the openings in the cane-bottomed chair at the design in the carpet or peeked through the slats of the chair-back at the figures in the wallpaper.

Occasionally, instead of making brief calls on shut-ins, we stopped at a church official's home for some talk about church business. I especially liked this because here we were usually served a cool drink and cookies, or when the weather was chilly cocoa-with-marshmallow and cake—or perhaps even chowder with crackers.

On the way home, in contrast to the way over, my father and I would talk. If it were still light enough, he would point out the beauties of nature. In early spring he called my attention to the delicate green of budding trees and the brave little blossoms peeping up beside the road. He showed me how to tell the difference between trees by their contours, the texture of their bark, and the shape of their leaves. Once he stopped and stripped off a small bit of slippery elm, giving me the moist inner bark to chew, as he said he had often done in his youth. And once he made me a birch whistle, carefully loosening the bark, whittling with his pocketknife an opening in the wood and angling its end, then slipping the bark over it again like a glove over a hand. Apparently this did not strike him as a desecration of the Sabbath! In summer the late afternoon coolness, in pleasant contrast to the scorching heat of the midday, made our returning drive a pleasure. In autumn the tangy smell of the air and the glow of the brilliant trees delighted us. No blight had yet killed the chestnut trees, which were plentiful in Connecticut, and sometimes on our homeward ride we would stop to gather the prickly burrs and pound them on a rock with our heels to dislodge the cluster of sweet chestnuts within.

One brisk autumn day my father talked to parishioners after the service longer than usual. Growing restless, I slipped out to wait for him in the buggy. It would be helpful, I decided, to get everything ready for us to start, so I untied the knot that secured the short rope to the hitching post. Then I climbed into the buggy and picked up the reins. The horse, as impatient as I, immediately started down the broad village street. I was terrified. I pulled on the reins in an effort to bring him to a stop but this only increased his speed. Soon we were tearing down the street, headed for the hill which led straight down to the river. Helplessly I sat on the edge of the seat, the reins in my hand and visions of disaster whirling through my head.

The wide steps of the village post office which was located on this street were a favorite gathering place for idle men, especially on Sunday. Those sitting there now saw the runaway horse, the hitching rope dangling from his bit, and the frightened little girl alone in the buggy. One of them—a tall young fellow, quicker than the others—jumped up, ran into the street, and with a leap caught the dangling rope. He pulled hard on it, bringing the horse to a stop. Holding the bridle, he talked softly to the animal and stroked his long neck to calm him.

As I sat back limply I saw through the tail of my eye my father coming running down the street. He was hatless and the tails of his Prince Albert coat flapped behind him. When he reached us he silently took the rope from the young man, then, recovering his breath and his dignity, shook hands with him and thanked him soberly. My rescuer rejoined his companions on the post-office steps. Father unclasped the hitching rope from the bit, placed it on the floor of the buggy, and climbed in. Without a word he took the reins from my hands and turned the horse around in the wide street. In silence we drove back to the church, where he stopped just long enough to get his hat and topcoat.

On the way home Father asked me if I realized how serious my adventure had been and how grateful I should be to the Lord—also to his agent, the young man—for my rescue. I nodded miserably and promised never again to touch the hitching rope unless he was beside me. I had often heard Father speak disapprovingly of the loafers on the post-office steps who, he thought, might better have been in church, but after this day I never heard them mentioned. I begged him not to tell my mother what had happened and perhaps he did not, for she never spoke of the incident to me. But for months I would sometimes wake in the middle of the night bathed in a cold sweat from dreaming that I was whirling down a broad street behind an uncontrollable horse, headed for certain destruction.

With the coming of winter there were fewer Sunday excursions for me. Once or twice, when the ground was covered with a hard-packed crust of snow and the sleighing was fine, I made the Sunday drive with my father in a cutter. Little more than my nose was exposed to the cold as I sat bundled in heavy winter clothes with extra shawls and scarves wound about me, my mittened hands tucked under the heavy blanket and my feet resting snugly on a well-wrapped hot flatiron. Veils of white steam poured from the horse's nostrils, the runners made a slippery, slithery sound, and the sleigh bells jingled merrily. My father did all the driving, for the cold weather made the horse frisky and a firm hand was required to guide him along the worn ruts of the icy road or turn him out from them when we met an oncoming sleigh. There was no studying of sermon notes on these rides and little conversation, but both my father and I were conscious of the frozen beauty around us and exhilarated by the smooth, swift motion of the sleigh.

By the time we arrived at the little church I would be feeling almost giddy from the cold air. I would peel off my extra layers of clothing and sit through the service in something of a stupor. On the ride home the rays of the setting sun were not even faintly warming, and the iron at my feet was stone cold. It was good to gain the shelter of the home kitchen and the comfort of a cup of hot cocoa.

Besides making the Sunday afternoon trip to preach, Father also went to his second parish once or twice or more during the week. Often he rode his bicycle and occasionally he walked the three and a half miles. Usually he conducted the midweek prayer meeting. He tried to keep in close touch with all members of his church, and frequently he made a special trip to consult with church officials on business and other matters connected with his second "charge."

One of the faithful members of the official board in this second parish was a lobsterman. He invited Father to go out any time with him on his boat when he went to haul lobster pots. Father thought this a good chance to talk over church affairs as well as to get a few hours of relaxation on the water. A difficulty was the fact that he sunburned easily and, in spite of anything he could do, after a few hours on the river in bright sunlight his nose would redden, peel, become unsightly and uncomfortably sore. "You look as if you had been patronizing one of the saloons you preach against," the boys teased him. This he took with a smile, but he disliked their suggesting that his presence was welcome on the lobster boat because it kept away the inspectors who roamed the river in their put-put boats looking for lobstermen who failed to put back undersized lobsters. It was true that no matter how informally my father dressed he still seemed to look like a minister, and that no boat he sat in was likely to have its catch examined. But Father resented the idea that his lobsterman church official would try to evade the law or would use his minister to play a part in such a performance.

Another of the official board members in the second church was a doctor with several children only a little younger than we were. He too had a power boat on the river, but this one was for pleasure, not business. Several times each summer we were invited to go for outings on this boat. They were high points in our summer, especially when we picnicked on an island some miles out in Long Island Sound.

At my father's second double charge the ride between parishes followed the course of the Connecticut River much of the way. At one point the road emerged from a woodsy stretch onto an open ridge from where there was an unobstructed view over the fertile valley with the broad, beautiful river flowing through it. Often on our homeward drive when we reached this highest point my father would stop the horse and we would sit and gaze. " 'Where rolls the bright Connecticut/In silver to the sea,' " he would quote, adding, "I remember hearing my mother say that when I was a little boy. I wonder where she got it."

To this day I do not know, but I can testify to the bright, silvery quality of the Connecticut River then, with the sun shining upon it as it made its way to the Atlantic.

Father often quoted poetry on our way home. Once he recited the Joaquin Miller poem about Columbus and after every "Sail on" asked me to identify the hero. To his disappointment and my chagrin it was not until the last stanza that I came up with the right answer. One spring, when our school class was learning the Wordsworth "Daffodil" poem, he asked me to teach it to him; strangely, he did not already know it. And I remember that a year later on one of these rides he suggested that we say it together. To my discomfiture I had forgotten most of the lines but he could recite the whole poem perfectly.

Among the members in this small church was an elderly childless couple who had a dog that was "family" to them. All day the dog followed one or the other around; he sat on his own chair between them at meals; at night he slept on the foot of their bed. When they attended my father's service in the little chapel on Sunday afternoon the dog decorously followed his master and mistress up the aisle and settled himself comfortably on the pew beside them.

At first this annoyed my father. He remarked that while he presumed he had preached to dogs before they had not been four-legged ones. But he was not a man to speak out on first impressions, and as he grew accustomed to the situation he admitted that it not only ceased to bother him; he even rather enjoyed it. No one in his congregation, he said, was quieter or better behaved than that dog.

The dog's mistress was an excellent cook, and she and her husband hospitably insisted on feeding the minister—and his daughter if she happened to be along—after the service. It was always a fine, hearty meal. One day, however, we hurried away without enjoying it because an urgent request had come for my father to call on a family living on the "lower road." This road ran along beside the river, a mile or so below the more traveled macadamed highway. It was a bad road to drive on, narrow and curving to follow the bends of the river. In summer its dirt surface sent up clouds of dust and in spring it was often submerged when the Connecticut overflowed. "Freshets," the river people called these spring floods. The people who lived in small cottages along the lower road were mostly "foreigners," lately arrived from southern Europe. For a living they fished or worked at odd jobs or in the old brownstone quarry a few miles down the river, and they pretty much kept to themselves. Most of them, it was assumed, were of the Roman Catholic faith.

On this day the water on the lower road came almost to the wheel hubs, and my father let the horse pick his own way through it. We stopped before a small unpainted cottage where two or three men leaned against the open door of the tar-covered kitchen lean-to. They looked up as Father got out but did not move. He handed me the reins, saying that after the heavy going the horse could be trusted to stand quietly and that he would try not to be gone long.

I watched him walk quickly to the open door and greet the men, one of whom took him inside the cottage. From some inner room I could hear a subdued murmur of conversation, partly in English and partly in some other tongue. Suddenly there came the sound of a woman weeping—loud, unrestrained sobs. And then I heard my father's voice—low, sympathetic, comforting. The sounds faded and all was still. In spite of the late afternoon sunshine I felt chilly and strangely disturbed.

My eyes followed the shadows of the moving elm branches as they wove patterns on the road ahead, and my ears caught the sound of the rippling waves sent by the full-flowing river to lap against its bank. A broken limb creaked in the breeze. I felt very much alone and a little afraid. My knees began to shake; I shivered, and my mouth became dry.

A car stopped behind me. Two policemen got out, pushed past the men at the door and went inside. I listened, but no sound came from the cottage. Each moment seemed to me like an hour. At last there was a movement at the door. Waves of relief flowed over me as my father emerged and shook hands with the men still standing beside the lean-to. I could see that his face looked strained and sad.

We drove awhile in silence. When we were safely beyond a badly flooded stretch of road he told me what had happened. "Their little girl was drowned," he said slowly. "She ran away and must have slipped down the riverbank. They searched for hours, then found her body caught on a tree branch half a mile down the river." He shook his head pityingly. For a time he did not speak. Then, his face troubled, he mused aloud, "I should have come down to the lower road long ago—before they had to send for me."

Suddenly to my father's surprise and to my own I began to cry. I sobbed uncontrollably, choked, and sobbed again. Father gave me his big handkerchief. He took one hand from the reins and patted my shoulder, saying, "There, there!"

That night, after only a few moments of rest, Father went to the church to occupy a pulpit for the third time that day. Mother did not go to the evening service. Instead, she stayed home to fix me a hot supper, after which she sent me off to bed.

For a long time I lay sleepless and troubled. That poor family! That poor little girl! The "bright Connecticut" rolling "in silver to the sea" had not been so bright that day. I felt a surge of anger against it, and as I finally fell asleep I wondered if ever again I could enjoy being on it or even near it.

8. Special Days and Holidays

Most of the year's special days and holidays were joyously celebrated in our home. New Year's was not really joyous but it was a special day, marked by promises and resolutions. For the adults of the family it was preceded by the midnight watchnight prayer service at the church. Yet there was no late rising the next morning, for all day on this first day of the year my father would be out making calls. This was an annual custom of his; several years he made close to a hundred calls between ten in the morning and ten at night. One year he left at each home a card he had had printed with his name and the greeting: "I wish you a year of prosperity, of health, of high purpose, of steady advance in all things good and noble."

At home Helen and I spent the morning helping Mother put the place in good order and prepare for the informal open house she held in the afternoon. Callers were served tea and cookies beside the still-standing Christmas tree. In spite of its glittering tinsel and ornaments it looked rather forlorn, for all its edible decorations were gone. Soon it would come down; soon too the Christmas school holidays would be over. Then we would start looking ahead to Easter and spring vacation, and before that to the celebration of three family birthdays—Rob's and Herbert's in February and Helen's in March.

Birthdays were a real event in our household. After the "Happy Birthday" shouts and the loudly protested spanking—really love pats, one for each year and one to grow on—came breakfast with its concealed shiny pennies, as many as the birthday required. They might be found beneath the place mat, the salt shaker, the knife, the water glass, the milk pitcher, within the rolled-up napkin. No chores today for the birthday boy or girl, and after school some sort of special treat. Or perhaps there might be a small birthday party with the young guests bringing inexpensive presents, playing favorite games, and enjoying the regulation finale of ice cream and cake. At supper the presents from members of the family, piled in the birthday person's chair, were fun to unwrap and discover. Something small, like a pencil, might be wrapped in layer after layer of paper and then placed in box after box with the last one as big as a hatbox. No gift cost more than a few pennies, but every one was exclaimed over as if it were worth a million. To top off the supper there was the birthday cake, the choice of the birthday person—sponge or spice, coconut or chocolate.

Helen's March birthday one year was celebrated with an unusual party. She chose to invite the dozen or so deaf mutes who attended Sunday morning service at our church, together with two of their teachers. She planned the games with care, using ones like "Hide the Thimble" and guessing games which did not depend on hearing or speech. The party was a great success. The children, their teachers said, were rarely invited into a home and all of them had a wonderful time. It was a big occasion for us too, as we adjusted to their handicap and marveled at their abilities and at their cheerfulness.

Easter, though a special day, was not altogether a happy one for my sister and me, due to Father's emphasis on its spiritual aspects. Although he approved of the church being decorated with flowers, he strongly disapproved of the congregation appearing in new Easter clothes. "Parading Easter finery," he felt, injected a worldly note into this significant religious occasion. Even if Helen and I had new or made-over spring dresses ready to wear we were not allowed to put them on on Easter Sunday. It was painful to us both to look around and see our friends and their elder sisters and their mothers all decked out in new spring outfits while we were wearing our old winter clothes. Neither did we have any colored Easter eggs or chocolate bunnies at home since Father thought these might take our minds off the true meaning of Easter.

Memorial Day, usually spoken of as Decoration Day, was in my childhood in New England a day devoted to paying tribute to the soldiers of the Grand Army of the Republic, both living and dead. The veterans of the Civil War were getting to be old men now, and each year there were fewer of them. More nearly than Easter, Decoration Day coincided with the coming of spring, for in our part of the country most spring-blossoming shrubs were not in full bloom until the latter part of May. Then the lilac bushes were usually at their best and their fragrance was all about. Father would find a reason for working in a part of his garden near a big lilac bush, since he loved this aroma. If Mother sent me to tell him that someone was waiting to see him she might add, "You know where to find him!"

Early on Decoration Day scores of schoolchildren brought armfuls of flowers to the basement of the town hall where a group of women waited to make them into small bouquets. For on this day a new flag and a fresh bouquet would be placed on the grave of every soldier buried in a cemetery within the township.

Father, being chaplain of the local Grand Army of the Republic, rode in a carriage with some of the G.A.R. officials. A few veterans rode in other carriages but all who were able proudly marched in their blue uniforms or in civilian garb behind the fife-and-drum corps and the flag-bearers. Following the veterans flocked the children, each carrying a small bouquet. With them Helen and I marched to the nearby cemetery where, like the other girls and boys, we placed our flowers on a soldier's grave beside the new flag already there. After the children sang a patriotic song the chaplain read a psalm and made a brief prayer and a bugler sounded taps while the veterans stood at attention.

The ceremony was repeated at a second in-town cemetery, then the children left and the veterans were taken in a bus to the several outlying graveyards. Returning to the town hall they were served lunch by the same ladies who had sorted the flowers. After a few brief speeches the old men went home for their afternoon naps while the women cleared up the big room. Memorial Day was certainly not a gay holiday, but it was one not quickly forgotten.

Between it and the Fourth of July came two family birthdays—mine and my father's. I remember once or twice having a small outdoor party with games under the trees and as a climax Mother's good homemade ice cream and cake. She laughed when in the middle of a game one small boy inquired, "When do we get the party?" Almost as good as a party was the special treat Mother planned another year. An ice-cream parlor on Main Street had a veranda overhanging the river, where they served customers. There my mother, my best friend of the moment, and I slowly sipped our chocolate ice-cream sodas through colored straws and watched the boats go up and down the river and the people and cars and horses and wagons cross the bridge which carried the Main Street traffic across the river.

The importance of Father's birthday, which came at the end of June, was somewhat dimmed by the fast-approaching glorious Fourth. Next to Christmas this was the most important holiday of the year, especially for the younger members of every family. In spite of frequent accidents, sometimes serious, fireworks were not then outlawed. Every family with children was expected to invest in a supply of firecrackers for daytime use and of fireworks to be set off after dark. In our family the children had to provide their own firecrackers since, as Mother hardly needed to tell us, the family budget did not have "money to burn." Just the same, we could count on Father's bringing home a big brown paper bag a few days before the Fourth and handing it somewhat sheepishly to Mother to put away. We all knew it held sparklers, pinwheels, Roman candles, and rockets for our Fourth-of-July evening.

No one expected to sleep much the night of July 3. At midnight church bells rang, giant firecrackers exploded, and cannon were fired to announce the arrival of the grand and glorious Day of Independence. And from midnight on, the noise continued. Our breakfast was eaten and family prayers endured to the accompaniment of our neighbors' firecrackers. Chores were speedily disposed of and the holiday was ours to enjoy. Sometimes we went on a family picnic but more often my brothers, taking their firecrackers with them, rushed off to join their friends, most of whom were better supplied. "Be very careful, boys," Mother would call after them, "and come home at noon."

Sitting on our side porch my sister and I tossed out small firecrackers which we had lighted from slow-burning sticks of punk. We would see how far we could throw the crackers and which ones, Helen's or mine, would pop the loudest. Sometimes Mother joined us and took her turn at lighting and throwing the lively little red crackers.

Our noon meal might have a special dessert but it would not be ice cream; that was reserved for evening. Before the boys rushed off again to an afternoon ballgame or wherever the excitement might be, Mother would corral one of them to chip ice from the block in our icebox and then turn the handle of the wooden two-quart freezer. Adding coarse salt to the layers of ice she would watch as the handle turned harder and harder, slower and slower. When it would scarcely turn at all she opened the container and took out the revolving dasher. As if on signal we children swarmed around to lick the paddle-like blades and sample the vanilla ice cream or lemon sherbet.

On this day we welcomed the coming of darkness. Then all of us gathered in our side yard, often joined by a few neighbors who brought their contributions to the evening fireworks. Between setting off the rockets and Roman candles, which Father and the boys manipulated, we would look up and admire the more lavish color displays made by bigger rockets which soared into the sky with a zoom, burst into a myriad of bright stars, then faded gently away as they fell toward earth. While distant rockets were still bursting in air, we enjoyed our ice cream or sherbet and cake. Watching the spectacular entertainment in the sky as we ate our holiday treat seemed an appropriate way to end our Independence Day celebration.

Walter's birthday, which fell in the sultry days of early August, was now less often celebrated at home than outside, with a group of friends. One year he rented a horse and two-seated carriage for the Saturday afternoon nearest his birthday and invited the girl he was fond of (and later married) and another young couple for a ride. For some reason—perhaps as a sort of concession to propriety

—I was asked to go along. I remember that I sat alternately in the front and the back seat. Presumably the close quarters necessitated by making room for a hefty eight-year-old girl did not bother any of them, and I remember my delight at being treated to strawberry ice cream at a soda parlor where we stopped.

After two uneventful months of school came the night of Halloween fun. This, I believe, was the one night of the year when my father would like to have ordered his sons to stay at home, but to his credit he did not. He did, however, deliver a lecture before they went out after supper, reminding them of their obligation as minister's sons to set good examples. Let him not hear of their being involved in any disgraceful act of hoodlumism or in any property damage or destruction!

On the broad rock at the top of the hill meadow where Helen and I picked daisies in June, a great pile of dry wood awaited a match. For several days not only teen-agers but some adults had lugged up the hill branches of dead trees, odd bits of lumber, parts of fences, even barn doors and sides of broken-down outhouses. Now in the early evening darkness a straggling youthful procession dragged up still more fuel, both licit and illicit, for the bonfire. Toward midnight, while some daring youths climbed a church steeple and set the bells to ringing, the flames of the hilltop fire blazed high into the sky. The day after Halloween brought outraged cries of protest about missing fences, barn doors, and privies, but to my parents' relief no connection was ever revealed between their sons and any acts of depredation.

Just as Father's birthday was eclipsed by the soon-to-follow Fourth, so was Mother's by Thanksgiving. This special day centered around the union church service in the morning and the big home dinner in the afternoon. Some years we had turkey, often the gift of a thoughtful parishioner; other years we were content with a couple of stuffed chickens. Mashed potatoes and yellow turnips, creamed onions, and cranberry sauce accompanied the *pièce de résistance,* and for dessert Mother made two kinds of pie —mince (*sans* liquor flavoring) and squash (preferred by many New England housewives to pumpkin). To fill any possible crevices a great bowl of apples, grapes, pears, raisins, and nuts ended the meal. It was a feast to remember—and to spend the rest of the day digesting. Except for doing the dishes, we did nothing beyond sitting around reading or playing quiet games. Unless, like Father, one chose to take a long walk.

From Thanksgiving on, our minds were fixed on the biggest and best holiday of the year—Christmas. Each of us made lists of gifts to be made (these were many) or bought (these were few). We also made a list of the things we wanted to receive and tacked it on the inside of a cupboard door which served as a family bulletin board. Evenings formerly devoted to reading, music, or games were now filled with industry. In the woodshed one of the boys was sure to be sawing or whittling to produce bookends, letter containers, a plant stand, or a hot-dish rack. Near the hanging lamp Helen and I bent over such projects as potholders overcast with bright yarn, penwipers created from discarded kid gloves, red-checked place mats cross-stitched in a simple design, pancake-style blotters, or small calendars attached with narrow ribbon to a series of picture postcards.

For morning prayers Father now read the familiar early chapters of Luke, and around the house he whistled or sang Christmas carols instead of hymns. Near the middle of the month we interrupted our evening work with sessions in the kitchen to prepare Christmas-tree trimmings. These would augment the tinsel and shining ornaments carefully kept from year to year. Over the fire in the big black range we popped corn in a wire popper and strung the fluffy white blossoms on long strings, every now and then putting in a cranberry for color. We ate the imperfect kernels —and it was surprising how many we found. We also tied red string around animal crackers, leaving short lengths to fasten them onto the tree. Naturally only perfect beasts could be used, and three-legged camels or other defective animals were quickly devoured. We tied red string, too, to a limited supply of candy canes and ribbon candy and to the stems of carefully selected, highly polished small red apples. We made loosely woven green string baskets to encase half a dozen oranges—a fruit almost nonexistent in our lives during the rest of the year. And we gilded the shells of a handful of English walnuts.

Before Christmas Mother made an extra-large baking of sugar cookies, using star and tree-shaped molds. Helen and I packed the best-looking of them in small boxes (we never threw away boxes) and took them to shut-ins.

A few days before Christmas my father and brothers, clad in

their warmest clothes, set out for a distant parishioner's woods. They carried an ax and hatchet and dragged a sled on which to bring back the family Christmas tree. "Choose a good one!" we directed them, and they always did. When mounted in its weighted wooden box and set in its place of honor in the parlor it stood sturdy and straight and tall enough to brush the ceiling. Now the box of tinsel and ornaments was brought down from the attic and the popcorn strings and other homemade decorations produced. We all had a hand in trimming the tree, and when it was done to everyone's satisfaction the double doors to the parlor were closed until Christmas morning.

In our household, surprisingly, stockings were never "hung by the chimney with care," neither do I remember any talk of a Santa Claus. All attention was concentrated on the tree. Gifts, secretly and not too skillfully wrapped in white tissue or even plain brown paper and tied with narrow red ribbon, yarn, or string, were carefully labeled and turned over to Mother. She, we knew, would add others, including the mysterious packages which arrived by mail from our out-of-town relatives, and see that all appeared as if by magic on or around the tree on Christmas morning.

Christmas morning was an exercise in self-restraint, for the surprises and joys which lay behind the closed parlor doors must wait until breakfast was eaten, prayers over, dishes done, and beds made. Then we all lined up, the youngest (me) in front, the oldest (Father) at the rear, each (except me) with hands on the shoulders of the one ahead. All over the house we marched, lustily singing Christmas carols. At last we stopped before the closed doors, burst them open with a shout, and entered upon our Christmas paradise. Now the branches of the beautiful tree were weighted down not only with the trimmings we had put there but with mysterious small packages, while all manner of larger ones were piled on the floor around the tree.

For an hour or more the happy flurry of unwrapping packages went on. Each of us enjoyed both the pleasure of receiving simple presents made with love or bought with hard-earned pennies, and that of watching others open our gifts to them. Sometimes we would find a treasure we had dreamed of possessing but hardly dared to hope for. Once it was for me a silver bracelet, and once a pair of skates. One year I had wanted a ring desperately. To my delight a small branch held a tiny package marked with my name. Excitedly I tore off the white tissue wrapping and found a red-velvet box just the right size for my longed-for ring! I could hardly contain my joy. Brimming with happy expectation I raised the lid and saw—a silver thimble. For a moment I stared at it in disbelief. Then I burst into tears and with an unusual display of temper threw the red-velvet box and its contents across the room.

Another year I looked all over the tree vainly searching for a package with my name on it. Had no one remembered me? Then in a corner of the room I saw a screen with a sign: EDITH'S TREE. Tearing away the screen I found a perfect little tree, perhaps only a foot and a half high, trimmed with tinsel and covered with tiny gifts—all for me. It was a sweet thought on my brothers' part to provide the tree and for Mother and Helen to deck it out so prettily. But I liked better being part of the family group and having my presents on the family tree, and never wanted the experience repeated.

Our Christmas dinner duplicated to a lesser degree our Thanksgiving one. After it we spent the day enjoying our new possessions—playing with our new games, reading our new books, reveling in our new treasures. If among the Christmas gifts there had been a sled or a pair of skates, and if the sliding on the nearby hill happened to be good or the skating safe on the nearby pond, these outdoor sports might well be substituted for indoor fun. The day ended with the family singing carols around the piano and feasting on popcorn, apples, and Christmas candy.

During the week following Christmas the edible decorations on the tree disappeared and early in the New Year the tinsel and ornaments were packed away and the tree taken down and chopped into firewood. Once again the round of schooldays, Saturdays, Sabbaths, special days, and holidays began. But all through the year the memory of Christmas, the very best of the year's special days, lingered on and continued to glow in our hearts.

9. Campmeeting Vacation

Ranking high among the year's special days were those of the annual August vacation. Each year the church freed Father from two and sometimes from three Sundays of preaching. He and Mother agreed that the vacation should be spent in some peaceful place conducive to building up physical and spiritual strength for the strenuous months to come. But they held different opinions as to the kind of place that should be. Father favored a rustic camp where we would live in tents, cook and eat our meals in the open, and at night sit around a campfire communing with sunset and evening star.

"Bugs! Mosquitoes! Rain! Shivering in the cold! Catching pneumonia from the damp ground! Never!" And Mother's vehement outburst quickly put an end to Father's idealistic vacation dream.

Martha's Vineyard was too far away and a cottage at the shore too expensive. There remained the Methodist campground in the heartland of Connecticut—a place of peace and quiet on a pine-covered hilltop. Here scores of small cottages were set close together on narrow dirt roads laid out in ever-widening circles around the large open-air "tabernacle." Many of the large cottages were owned and maintained by churches in the district; most of these were in or near the "inner circle." Other cottages were occupied by owners or renters, many of them ministers and their families, some for the whole summer, some for just a few weeks, and a few for only the last two weeks of August when first Chautauqua lectures and then religious meetings were scheduled.

An agent handled the renting of cottages by the week or month, the modest prices varying according to size, condition, and location. Some renters wanted to be near the tabernacle; others preferred being handier to the sanitary facilities set up in several places just beyond the outermost circle; it was also quieter there. Some cottages were piped for the excellent Artesian well water; other cottage occupants had to carry their water by the pailful from the pumps which were placed at convenient locations around the grounds. Mother and Father made their choice from those cottages available for August and paid the required deposit.

July was a busy month for Father for this month his church played host to the members of the Congregational church while its minister was on vacation. In August while my father was away the roles would be reversed, with the Methodists worshiping in the Congregational church. Besides preaching for his Congregational colleague in July Father also took over many of his pastoral duties—marriages, funerals, calling on the sick. In return, the Congregational minister would do the same for him in August.

Parsonage activities in late July began to resemble those before a move to a new parish. Clothes were washed and ironed and set aside ready to pack, the good silverware was secreted in the attic and food staples put into tins against marauding mice and ants. Mother planned the meals for the final week so that nothing would be left over and baked extra bread, cookies, and cake to take with us, for vacation cottage ovens were rarely usable. Before leaving, Father made a last round of calls on the sick; he also stopped in every store where we had an account and paid whatever was owed, for it was a point of honor with him not to leave town with a single debt unpaid, no matter how small.

One trunk, Mother decided, would have to do for the duration of the vacation. Into it went a selection of books for individual reading and for reading aloud, a dozen or so sermon envelopes my father insisted on taking, games, bed and table linen, every-day silver, and kitchen utensils. When Mother finished there was not room for a thimble, and the expressman groaned as he man-euvered the trunk out to his wagon.

Suitcases—one apiece—held personal clothing and possessions. This still left the well-wrapped tin breadbox, filled with bread, cake, and cookies, another box containing a few jars of canned fruit and jelly, and our outside wraps. Besides, of course, the box lunch to be eaten on the train. How we managed to get all these things to the station and onto the train I don't know, but we did. Some years one or two of my brothers was there to help, but more often they had other vacation plans and there were only my parents, my sister, and me. To make matters worse, we had to change trains midway on the trip. Naturally we ate our lunch before the change so there would be one less package to carry; still, it was no mean feat to get ourselves off one train and onto another without leaving anything behind or losing anything on the way.

During the early part of the train ride Mother, who was a chronic worrier, would sit with her eyes closed—resting, she said, but we all knew she was trying to think of something she might have forgotten to do or to bring. Father was relaxed and taking pleasure in pointing out to Helen and me features of the land-scape—a high viaduct, an expanse of evergreens, a rippling river, a well-kept farm, Brother So-and-So's church spire dominating some small town.

After the train ride a ten-minute trolley trip brought us to the foot of the campground hill. Father trudged up it and returned with a boy pulling a handcart. Helen and I scampered up the hill ahead of the others and the loaded cart. We passed under the rustic arch which spanned the campground entrance and waited at the edge of an area shaded by giant oaks and sweet-smelling pines whose browned needles carpeted the uneven ground. At the office near the gate Father picked up our key. We passed the roofed-over tabernacle platform and the semicircular sea of wooden benches facing it. We noted that the bookshop, bakery, and restaurant across the way were closed but that the small grocery store was open for business.

Turning ino a narrow curved street we soon crossed the wobbly porch of our vacation home and entered the small front room. It was sparsely furnished with a somewhat unsteady table, a few chairs, and a battered couch. The smaller back room held a wooden table and chairs and a kerosene stove. Upstairs were one small and two smaller bedrooms.

Not until Mother had inspected the mattresses and looked in every corner to be sure the place was entirely clean and insectless would she allow the suitcases to be carried upstairs. Everything being in order, she gave Father a list and sent him on a trip to the store while she, Helen, and I unpacked suitcases and put fresh linen on the springless beds.

The next morning the trunk arrived and was unpacked, neighbors and friends dropped in to welcome us, and Helen and I made short excursions to every corner of the little settlement. Soon our days took on a kind of pattern—late breakfast, prayers, chores, freedom until the simple hearty noon meal, then naps, visiting, a few hours in the open, light supper, an evening of games or reading, and early bedtime.

Nearly every afternoon while Mother sat with her sewing on the little front porch, often in the company of some other minister's wife, Father would take a long walk through the neighboring countryside. Sometimes he went alone, sometimes with one or two of his minister friends, and often with one or both of his daughters.

Those walks! There was nothing hurried about them. We stopped often to look, to listen, to touch. A lovely tree, a flowering meadow, a cloud-banked sky, a cluster of hazelnuts clinging to a stone wall, the sudden call of a bird from a thicket of white birches, a tiny stream murmuring on its way over its rocky bed —none of these things escaped Father, nor would he let them escape us. Something might recall an incident of his youth on the farm which he would share with us with great relish. Or the lines of a poem might come all unbidden to his lips.

Occasionally instead of a nap and a walk or visit with neighbors after the mid-day meal we would stroll together along a wooded trail which led to a secluded grove. "The great trees rest me,"

Father remarked, and looking up at the tall pines he would quote: " 'The murmuring pines and the hemlocks . . . ,' " then stop, expecting us to complete the verse. He would stretch out on a cushiony bed of fragrant pine needles for his afternoon nap while the rest of us read or explored or just sat and talked quietly together. Later, propping our backs against the straight firs, my mother, sister, and I would take turns reading aloud, laughing at Father, who, as he listened attentively, tried to pace up and down on the uneven ground made slippery by the pine needles.

As the week of the Chautauqua meetings drew near more people arrived, upsetting the restful quiet of the grove. Nearly all of the cottages were occupied now, and the proportion of strangers increased. A line of parked carriages and cars stood outside the entrance arch. The bakeshop opened, and a few days later the restaurant. The series of Chautauqua programs were of "a high moral tone," with historical and biographical subjects predominating—all planned to stimulate one's intellectual life. Each evening some speaker of national note lectured in the open-air tabernacle, attracting large audiences.

The following week the meetings took a more religious turn. There were daily eventide song services in the larger cottages on the inner circle. A popular twilight song service was held in an open field just west of the grove, at the foot of a great boulder known as Sunset Rock, and hymn after hymn was wheezed out on a baby organ someone laboriously dragged to the field. Always as the colors of the setting sun spread over the western sky the service ended with the quiet singing of "Day Is Dying."

The campground bookstore was open now, its cramped quarters crowded with books which overflowed onto long tables outside its door. I pored over them but could find nothing to interest me, for the display was intended to appeal principally to ministers. Beyond the book tables was a table equipped with campstools and intended for the use of visitors who wanted to write a card or letter to the folks back home. At intervals along the table raw potatoes were placed to serve as holders for inky pens.

Each morning at the back door of the restaurant one could see a group of young men, mostly ministers' sons, peeling bushel after bushel of onions and potatoes. Some years the group included my brother Rob, and knowing his aversion to onions we thought this a good joke. We were glad, however, to make use of his employee's

Helen, Herbert, Robert, and Walter

Schoolroom in Mystic, Conn.

Edith

Parsonage at Thompsonville, Conn.

Summer Vacation at the Campground
Standing: Father, Helen, Edith
Seated: Members of Portland Epworth League, Mother (*center*), Robert

Edith and Aunt Sarah

privilege of buying for home consumption at less than restaurant-table prices such standard items as clam chowder, beef stew, and rice pudding.

With the beginning of the regularly scheduled religious meetings my sister and I were required to attend at least two of them each day, for it would not be fair, our parents told us, to enjoy the campground privileges without supporting its main reason for being. Since Rob had added to his restaurant job that of playing the cornet for the half hour of singing which preceded one of the several early evening meetings, Helen and I selected this service as one of the required two. The other was an afternoon religious-education class where because of our thorough training in the Scriptures we felt quite at home.

Delegations began arriving daily from various parishes in the area. Usually they stayed at the large church-owned cottages near the tabernacle, but if any persons from either of Father's two parishes came only for a single day they were entertained in our small cottage. There was now little time for walks or picnics, for both our parents were enlisted to lead devotional services or take on other responsibilities.

One afternoon after some meeting or other Mother was standing in a receiving line of ministers' wives set up to greet visitors. Suddenly, she told us, she heard a loud squeal and a hearty voice shouting, "That's my minister's wife! That's my minister's wife!" Turning, she saw the shining black face of one of my father's parishioners. Affectionately known as Aunt Josephine, she was made welcome and at home not only in many women's kitchens but also in her church. As Aunt Josephine continued proudly to point out her minister's wife Mother stepped out of the line, greeted her warmly, and to her great delight introduced her to a few of the ministers' wives. Learning that she had come in a bus with a church group from a neighboring community Mother made certain that she was sure of a place in it on the return trip. If there had been any doubt of this Mother would have brought Aunt Josephine home; like my father, Mother made no distinctions on color grounds.

All year long Sunday morning service was the high spot in Aunt Josephine's week. Dressed neatly in her best, she sat near the front and during the singing held high her most precious possession—a hymnal which she had bought and paid for herself. Father had ordered it for her, and when it arrived it had on its four corners manila cardboard protectors. These continued to protect the book, for Aunt Josephine never removed them. She carried the hymnal home with her, bringing it proudly to church each Sunday. Whether she held it right-side-up or, as some said, often upside down, its four cream-colored corner protectors were conspicuously present; it would have broken her heart to have lost one of them.

Still more people arrived at the campground when prominent preachers began appearing on the high wooden platform of the tabernacle every evening, and at some of the daytime meetings as well. A few of the oldtimers in the campmeeting deplored the absence of the fervor of bygone years. Then "outpourings of the spirit," they said, had been more evident. They recalled with relish dramatic outbursts, physical gyrations, and religious ecstasies and were sure that when they disappeared something tremendous had been lost. Most people, however—and this included our parents—preferred the calmer atmosphere which prevailed in our time. Not that religious fervor was entirely absent. There was still a kind of electric atmosphere in the soul-saving sessions which followed many sermons, when "hymns of invitation" were sung to entice sinners forward and preachers walked up and down the aisles to talk and pray with penitent persons.

The climax of the meetings came with the big Campmeeting Sunday at the end of August. On this day throngs of people arrived by trolley, train, car, and carriage. With difficulty they found places outside the arch to leave their private conveyances and poured into the campground, filling to overflowing the hundreds of tabernacle benches. After listening to special music and a sermon preached by a well-known bishop or missionary some of the visitors flocked to the restaurant, standing in line and keeping it crowded for hours. Others ate picnic lunches on the tabernacle benches or in some pleasant, shady spot on the outskirts of the ground. Afterward the visitors wandered about, attended one of the many afternoon meetings, and toward night started homeward, leaving the place littered and its occupants thankful for the return to comparative quiet.

Usually there were a few days of grace after the end of the meetings before we had to start for home. During this time Father would indulge in a few extra-long walks into the country.

On one of these walks I was with him when he spied, just inside a fenced-in country place, a tree loaded with ripe early fall apples. Many of them lay on the ground, some of them outside the fence. "I'm sure no one would begrudge us a few fallen apples," my father said, "but to be on the safe side, I'll ask." He walked up the path, knocked on the side door, and made his request to the housewife who answered his knock. To his amazement she refused him abruptly, shutting the door in his face.

Much chagrined, he turned and came slowly down the walk. "The answer is 'No,' " he said as he closed the gate carefully behind him. "But"—stooping to pick up a few apples outside the fence—"this—and this—and this—are, I believe, in public domain." Wondering if the ungenerous housewife might set a dog on us, we continued our walk down the country road, munching our first fall apples.

The autumn wind was beginning to whistle through the trees and the air was starting to grow chilly. The bookstore, the bakery, and the restaurant were shuttered for the winter, the empty tabernacle benches looked forlorn, most of the cottages were closed, and nearly all of our campground friends had left. With the grove beginning to take on the air of a deserted village we had few regrets as we packed our belongings, locked the cottage, and departed on our homeward journey.

"We return," my father wrote in his journal the next day, "strengthened physically and, I trust, spiritually." It had been a good month—one which we would not be sorry to repeat the next year.

10. "A Penny Saved . . ."

Money did not flow like water in our house. In fact, it did not flow at all. Our unit of currency was not today's dollar or yesterday's quarter or dime, but the lowly nickel and the Indianhead copper penny. Often we heard such sayings as "Money does not grow on trees," "Take care of the pennies and the dollars will take care of themselves," and "A penny saved is a penny earned." Thrift was not then considered unfashionable, and nowhere was it practiced more vigorously than in our home.

Fortunately my mother was an extremely good manager. She was painstakingly careful in all household matters, including her purchases and preparation of food. In buying staples she saved by purchasing in quantity and during sales. She had a knack of finding special buys; when she learned that broken crackers were sold at a reduced price in a cracker factory not far from my brothers' school she commissioned the boys to bring home a large bag of them once a week. Never did we have such extravagances as strawberries or lettuce out of season. Whatever was in greatest abundance and therefore cheapest was our meat—or vegetable, or fruit. Not knowing the difference between pot roast and roast beef we did not complain about pot roast, nor about having chuck instead of sirloin. Regular food purchases were made at the less expensive stores—not chain stores then—except that church loyalty required trading with a Methodist merchant wherever possible.

In her cooking as well as in her buying Mother was economically minded. When a recipe called for two eggs she used one; when it called for cream she used milk. "Peel the potatoes thin, daughter," was an admonition I heard often. Potatoes, being both nutritious and cheap, were served at almost every meal but in different ways so we would not tire of them. Bakers' bread was an unheard-of luxury. Twice a week Mother baked a batch of bread—several loaves of white and two of the graham preferred by Father. In the summer she filled dozens of Mason jars with the beans, peas, corn, and tomatoes Father raised in his big garden, and in the fall put up bushels of peaches and pears and filled dozens of small jars with jelly made from crabapples, grapes, plums, and quinces.

Mother was a great list-maker. Week by week she built up a list of clothing and other major family needs, then would go to a nearby city every three months or so on a shopping expedition. As I grew older she would often take me with her. I enjoyed going, but her thoroughness irritated me. Before buying a coat or material to make a dress she would go to half a dozen stores. She would feel the cloth and go to the door to see it in daylight and figure how she could do with a quarter of yard less than the clerk suggested. If she were buying a hat she would not hesitate to ask what the price reduction would be if she substituted for its present trimming her own feather or ribbon or jet ornament. When she finally made up her mind on some major purchase she would say, "I'll take it," with a worried sigh, as if she were settling the fate of nations.

Father was just as careful about money matters as Mother.

When he went to a preachers' meeting or to the annual church Conference, or to visit his brother in his Connecticut home town or his sister near there, he kept track of every penny he spent and after his return entered all expenditures in his journal. He would often ride on the "electrics" instead of the train to save the small difference in fares, and in getting on or off a train or boat would always carry his own suitcase rather than use a porter. Though fastidious about his appearance, Father was very conscious of the cost of clothing. He had to be! He relied on Mother's instinct for discovering sales or seasonal reductions and took advantage of them. He liked her to go with him to select a suit or overcoat but could do very well by himself.

All of us children knew that thrifty ways were not just important but essential. We knew that it was not easy for our parents to provide the kind of home they coveted for their children, with nourishing food, respectable clothing, and cultural advantages. Father's salary was far lower than that of most heads of families in the "upper middle class" bracket to which it was taken for granted a minister's family belonged. In order to feed his family economically he spent many hours cultivating a large garden. He also bought wood by the half cord and sawed and split it into stove-length pieces. Neither of these activities seemed to the community beneath a minister's dignity, and luckily my father enjoyed doing them. Incidentally he claimed that the ideas for some of his best sermons came to him in the garden or at the woodpile.

The rigid economy practiced by the minister's wife was also taken for granted. The hours she spent ironing the stiffly starched white shirts a minister was expected to wear in the pulpit went unnoticed, but she must also contribute her pot of beans to the church supper and make aprons to sell at the church fair. The ministers' sons might mow lawns, peddle newspapers, or deliver groceries but must not take a really dirty job; that would be a reflection on the church.

Few people either in or out of the church realized what a struggle it was for the minister's family to maintain the appearances demanded of them. It was assumed that somehow they could live on a high cultural and social level on a next-to-nothing income. They were also expected to do without high-priced modern conveniences such as electricity or, sometimes, a bathroom. If the old stove smoked or the aged faucet leaked let the minister's wife send one of the children to the Ladies Aid parsonage committee chairman, who would eventually send the least expensive repairman to try to correct the trouble.

We parsonage children were well aware that with the church people things that showed came first. A parsonage bedroom with peeling wallpaper was far less likely to be repapered than the front parlor which did not need it nearly so much, and the church would get a coat of paint long before the parsonage kitchen would have a much-needed sink. Inadequate heat in the upstairs study might compel the minister to sit at his desk in his overcoat, but that overcoat must look eminently respectable when he appeared in it on the street. The high cost of paper might lead him to make his sermon notes on scrap paper, but his pastoral notebook must not look shabby when he drew it from his pocket in public. And we, the minister's family, must be content with the least costly foods and keep—or at least look—warm without, sometimes, heavy enough winter coats. Nor must we complain. A minister's —and his family's—outlook on life should be spiritual, not materialistic!

Even as small children we were dimly aware of these things, though they did not bother us much and we did not often think about them. The lack of money did not, as a rule, weigh heavily on us. Sometimes we wailed when we were denied something we had set our heart on, though we knew very well that wailing would do us no good. But we never doubted that we would get what was needful—and sometimes a little more. For instance, there was the bag of unshelled peanuts Father almost always brought us after an out-of-town trip (even though he perhaps went without a lunch to do so). It was a family ritual for him or Mother to dole them out, a pile for each of us, with the "nubbins" (the stubby shells which held only a single nut) separately allotted with equal fairness.

We children took it for granted that most of our companions would have more spending money than we had. When my sister and I persuaded our parents to increase our small allowances to make them a little more like those of our friends, mine went up from five to ten cents a week. Later it was fifteen cents, and in high-school days a quarter. Out of this it was understood that all small personal indulgences must come, as well as a weekly contribution to the church. Our share of work around the house was to be done without payment, but we were paid for extra tasks. Killing flies, also potato bugs, brought a penny a hundred. (Counting the dead bodies and placing them in piles of ten was part of the deal.)

Sorting out the specked apples in a barrel was worth a nickel. Those apple barrels, which stood in the cellar, were testimony to Father's faith in the apple-a-day saying. Every fall he would lay in several barrels of good-keeping (he hoped) winter apples. Some years he would manage a trip to his brother's Farmington farm where he would spend the better part of a couple of days picking apples and putting them into barrels to be freighted to him. Some years, when apples were scarce and therefore high-priced, he had to pay what seemed to him an outrageous price. One year he paid six dollars for a barrel of Baldwin apples—plus thirty-five cents for delivery. "The most I have ever paid," he noted in his journal, "but *they are good!*"

Besides being eaten more or less freely by all of us, Mother used "Father's apples" for applesauce, baked apples, brown Betty (a popular dessert with the family, made with alternate layers of sliced apples and bread crumbs and seasoned with brown sugar and cinnamon), and—rarely—for pie. Almost every evening after Father had been working an hour or two in the study he would go down to the cellar and return with a plateful of apples which he would eat with great relish. As spring approached many of them were less suited for eating than for cutting up for cooking.

Besides his faith in the healthfulness of apples, Father believed that boneset tea was beneficial to "clear the blood" in early spring. At his insistence, Mother would brew a pot of the bitter tonic and let it stand on the back of the stove. To encourage us to drink it, Father would pay a penny for every cupful of the nasty stuff we swallowed. Grateful for a new source of pin money, we would hold our noses, gulp it down, and collect our pennies.

Father also rewarded us for something quite different—for memorizing certain psalms, the Ten Commandments, the Beatitudes, and a few other portions of the Bible. Mother, not to be outdone, paid us a nickel for learning the books of the Old Testament in order and another for the New. I remember going about the house chanting: "Genesis, Exodus, Leviticus . . . Matthew, Mark, Luke, John." To encourage us to read a simply written history of the United States, Father offered five cents. I thought I had discovered a perpetual source of income by continuous rereadings, but this was quickly disallowed.

More money was to be earned outside than at home. From their newspaper routes my brothers put something into a "higher education" fund as well as paying part of the cost of their bicycles and their musical instruments and providing themselves with skates, hockey sticks, baseball gloves—and candy. A secondhand printing press they were given and which they set up in the cellar and learned to use brought in considerable income as they developed a nice little business in printing personal cards, handbills for neighborhood stores, and programs for church and school-club affairs.

My sister and I found fewer outside earning opportunities than our brothers. Baby-sitting was not then a usual paid teen-age activity—parents either stayed at home with their small children or took them along when they went out in the evening. We could often earn a nickel or a dime wheeling a baby carriage after school when a young mother would entrust her baby, overconfidently perhaps, to a fairly young girl for an hour's airing. Selling Larkin products from door to door provided a more ambitious way to earn some desired object. Housewives were glad to buy in this convenient manner soaps and cleaning powders, coffee and tea, extracts and spices from the long list of Larkin Company products. Helen and I, being minister's children, had an advantage over most of our friends and could easily fill our order blanks, mostly at Methodist homes. In this way we earned such desirable premiums as a croquet set, a hammock, and a lawn swing for our side yard and a desk and table for indoors.

Our family's whole way of life exemplified the principle that "a dollar saved is a dollar earned." Carpets became rugs; tablecloths, place mats; the life of a worn sheet was extended by stitching outside selvage edges together or by fashioning the stout parts into pillowcases. Half-worn garments were declared "good for a few more wears," and nothing was discarded until its last possibility of use was exhausted. A dress might become a waist (blouse) or a skirt a petticoat, and the few pieces that survived these uses intact ended life in a patchwork quilt. Nothing must be wasted. And to both parents this applied to time as well as to food or clothes or money. "Time," said Father, "is one of our most precious possessions. Never let me hear you speak of 'killing time.' That is one of the wickedest expressions in the language."

A large box of slightly used clothing which arrived semiannually from Mother's "well-off" sister was often the starting point for a handing-down process. Many such garments made their way to me via my mother and sister. When I resented being their third or fourth owner Mother would say reprovingly, "This is a much better dress than we could buy you; you should be happy to have it."

Once, when I was perhaps eleven or twelve, I exclaimed that I would rather have a brand new gingham dress than all the made-over silk dresses in the world. My vehemence must have made an impression on my mother, for soon afterward she gave me the exact amount of money needed to buy enough yards of gingham to make a dress and told me I might go alone to select the material. To my delight she approved the blue-and-white checked material I selected and promptly made me a dress from it. That dress, one of my few really new ones, was a joy to me.

With five children and the church work which was expected of her—and which she enjoyed doing—extra household help was a necessity. It was held to a minimum, however, with Mother insisting on having a full-time helper only when the children were small. Even then she did a great deal of the housework herself.

When we graduated to part-time help, a sturdy woman arrived each Monday morning to handle the heavy part of the weekly wash. Since daybreak the fire in the kitchen stove had been going full tilt, heating water in the big copper boiler on top and in the tank within. The boys had brought up the wooden tubs from the cellar and had strung clotheslines in the back yard. After breakfast and family prayers were over and dishes done, the kitchen became transformed into a hot, steamy laundry, unless the day was fine and warm, when the tubs were set up outside. The corrugated rubbing board, the wringer attachment which fitted on the side of the tub, the long-handled dipper, bars of yellow soap, bottles of bluing, boxes of starch—all were part of the washday ritual. Gradually the yard became a maze of sheets and pillowcases, towels and washcloths, tablecloths and napkins tossing in the breeze alongside all sorts of wearing apparel. After school Helen's and my task was to unpin the clean-smelling articles from the line, dump them into the big clothes basket, and carry it to the kitchen for Mother to sort and fold.

Ironing usually was sandwiched in between other duties on other days of the week. It took a hot fire to heat the half dozen flatirons on the stove top, so the ironing board was set up some distance away. Nearly everything needed ironing. Mother did the difficult pieces, Helen helped iron simpler things, and I did place mats, napkins, and handkerchiefs.

When my brothers were in high school, college catalogs began appearing in the mail, together with letters enclosing estimates of yearly college expenses. The boys pored over them, and Father and Mother looked thoughtful. College education, it was clear, would be a drain on the family exchequer far beyond the small amount it had been possible to set aside in the "higher education" fund. Yet they were determined that every member of the family should have as much schooling as he or she desired.

An informal family council was held in which Father and Mother told us of their ambition for us and that to accomplish it we would all have to "put our shoulders to the wheel." Walter informed us of his decision not to go to college; he was learning the fundamentals of the printing business and wanted to continue with his work. Herbert and Rob definitely wanted a college education, and later there would be the two girls to think about. Herbert and Rob said they expected to work during the long vacation and perhaps during the college year too. In addition, the possibility of long-term outside loans was discussed.

Herbert was chosen to be valedictorian of his high-school class and of course everyone in the family wanted to go to his graduation. The train schedules were not cooperative in getting us the several miles to New London where his and Rob's school was, in time for the evening performance and back again after it. Besides, so many fares would add up to a considerable amount. After some deliberation Father and Mother decided to "splurge," and to hire for the evening a carriage with room for nine, drawn by a span of horses.

I was to go with the rest and I looked forward to the occasion with mounting excitement. For weeks I had been following along on Herbert's many-paged "oration" as he practiced it daily, prompting him when he hesitated. Now I would hear him deliver it from a real platform! This besides the fun of riding behind two horses and going to a theater for the first time—a practice contrary to our parents' belief but seemingly unavoidable in this case.

On the big evening the seven members of our family, our Aunt Sarah, and a special friend of Herbert's filled the conveyance and

Father drove the spirited span with ease and obvious enjoyment. From our seats at the front of the balcony we saw Herbert come in with his class and sit in the front row on the big stage. When he rose to deliver his oration I sat on the edge of my seat mouthing every word along with him. Had he stumbled I'm sure I would have shouted out the next word, but he did not. When he finished, I was too exhausted to applaud with the others.

The next day my only regret was that I had fallen asleep on the way home and so had failed to savor every moment of the midnight ride.

Such extravagances as the graduation evening outing were rare, but oh, so memorable! And of course this one could be justified in my parents' minds since it celebrated an important step along the way toward achieving the family's "higher-education" goals.

11. Parsonage Guests

———◆◆◆———

Many people dropped in at our parsonage home for a call, for a meal, for overnight, or even for several nights. An extra person or two made little difference in a household with five children and their parents and, much of the time, a "helper."

All three doors—front, side, and back—saw hard service. The back door, which led out to the woodshed and, lacking inside facilities, to the essential building at the rear, was used by delivery boys, peddlers, and tramps. Each morning, following the usual small-town food-shopping routine at that time, a grocery clerk came for the order he would deliver in the afternoon. Men and women wanting to sell soaps, pencils, shoelaces, and brushes came to this door, as did rug-selling Armenians with small rugs draped over their shoulders, and Slavic women carrying baskets of hand-made laces and embroideries to display and sell.

Back-door callers also included interesting town "characters." An elderly member of Father's church who kept a few hens would turn up every week or so to sell us a dozen eggs. He always priced them at an uneven figure and he never had with him more than half a dozen. These he would leave, collecting the money—including the extra half cent—and later in the day would return with the other half dozen—for which he again collected an extra half cent. We speculated that he wore out a penny's worth of shoe leather with his "Yankee" trick, but he probably considered himself a very shrewd businessman. Another back-door character, whom we saw only in the berry season, lived in a cabin on an outlying hill known as Rattlesnake Mountain. He brought around delicious blueberries he picked there and which he sold for eight cents a quart, two quarts for fifteen cents, or three for a quarter. Naturally Mother bought four quarts, even if she needed only three.

During times of widespread unemployment many tramps stopped at our back door to ask for food. Some of them were really down on their luck and needed a helping hand; others were idlers or adventurers. My mother would never deny one of them a couple pieces of buttered homemade bread, but that was as far as she would go. Begging was something not to be encouraged; besides, food was too precious in our house to do more. One day she saw a tramp throw away the bread-and-butter sandwich when he failed to find meat in it. After this, Mother insisted that any tramp who accepted the buttered bread eat it on the spot—along with a glass of water she would get him. If my father happened to be around he would make the man work for food, promising to give him a meal in return for a half hour's wood-chopping. The offer had few takers.

Our side door was the one commonly used by the family for its comings and goings, by young friends, and by the neighbors. Men selling subscription sets of books came here, and so did young men taking magazine subscriptions. In summer many college students who were going about selling aluminum cooking utensils—then something new—came to it. One sales method they used was to persuade a housewife to invite a few neighbors into her kitchen for a cooking demonstration, for which she would receive an aluminum pot or pan. My mother built up quite a collection of aluminum ware by letting college youths demonstrate its virtues by stewing tomatoes on her stove!

Afternoon callers ordinarily arrived at the front door, as did wedding couples, visiting clergymen, and other dignitaries. And from here, on a Sunday morning, the family emerged sedately bound for church. Since we had no telephone, if the Congregational minister wanted to arrange a union service he must stop by to talk it over. So must the young man desiring to engage Father's services for a marriage, and the undertaker needing them for a funeral. When ladies of the parish called on Mother in the afternoon they always used the front door. If the call were a casual one she might take the woman into the sitting room and perhaps even resume her mending as they talked. If it seemed more formal, she would usher the lady or ladies into the parlor and might even serve them tea.

Father received his callers in the study, carefully closing the door to insure complete privacy. We children, who usually answered the doorbell, came to have a sort of sixth sense about the people who asked for the minister. We suspected that the shy young man had come to arrange a wedding; that the unknown dignified gentleman was a clergyman from outside our area; that the troubled-looking youth wished to talk over some emotional problem with his pastor; and that the swaggering down-at-the-heels fellow was very likely an impostor bent on borrowing a little money.

Many men and some women who were having a hard time gravitated to the parsonage, assuming that a minister would be a kind-hearted easy mark. Father was certainly kindhearted, but he was no easy mark. He would listen to their stories, which might be genuine or might be brazenly concocted with the idea of getting a quick handout, and then he would ask revealing questions. When these upset the stories, as they frequently did, it did not take the caller long to find an excuse for leaving. If the person's request was for carfare to take him to some neighboring place where he claimed to have relatives, Father would ask for their name and address in order, he said, to alert the Methodist minister there to help. Usually Father would dig into his pocket and give the man the carfare—an act of generosity which he could ill afford. Calling it a loan, he would request its speedy return. Such "loans" were, however, seldom repaid.

One day an East Indian caller asked Father for help, and he

named a church mission in India with which he said he had been connected. By strange coincidence that very day a returned missionary from that part of India happened to be a parsonage guest. Father called him into the study and let him talk to the man. When his story fell completely apart, the East Indian beat a hasty retreat.

Monday morning was a favorite time for ministers of the area to drop in for a friendly call on Father. Then what more natural than to invite the caller to stay for dinner with the family? In this way we children came to know many of our father's ministerial associates. One guest we especially enjoyed because of the humorous stories he told. "When we moved to this last place," he told us, "I said to the ladies that my wife and I would certainly enjoy the parsonage facilities for we hadn't had a bath for three years." He chuckled and went on, "They looked so horrified that I hastily added *room* to the bath." When he went to live in a small Cape Cod town he said he asked a member of the church if this was a praying community. "Oh, yes," the man answered. "In winter we pray in the church and in summer we prey on the tourists."

Not all of our mealtime guests were drop-ins, but the evening meal was more likely to be specified for one invited ahead of time. This was both more leisurely and easier for Mother to prepare. In the fall she made a point of having each of her children's teachers for a company supper. This, she felt, was one way of establishing close relations between the home and the school. She paid no attention to our objection that this looked like an effort to "butter up" the teacher; she made us take a written invitation to the teacher and bring back her reply. The meal would be carefully prepared and nicely served, with everyone on his and her best behavior. But it was never really an enjoyable time, either for the one whose teacher was being entertained or, I am sure, for the teacher.

In the evening, by front or side door, young people often happened in to enjoy music or play games. Our parents encouraged the boys to invite their friends to the parsonage; this prevented outside exposure to card-playing or dancing—both strictly forbidden. Helen was always ready to play the piano for a "sing," and Mother was always agreeable to setting up a game of "Donkey," our playing-card substitute. If the guests were boys they often preferred to use the popular carom board.

We had many overnight guests, and some who stayed for a longer period. This involved a change in sleeping arrangements, since our guest room was usually occupied by one of the family. But it never occurred to our hospitable parents to object to making up a fresh bed or to the boys, who were usually the ones most affected, to fuss about doubling up or sleeping on a couch.

Many of our visitors were connected in some way with the church. Once every three months our presiding elder came to conduct the quarterly conference of the official board. He was always a welcome guest, and we were sorry that his visits were generally limited to a single night. Although most of his day was spent with Father in the study or out with him walking and talking and calling on important members of the parish, he always found time to chat with us children. He would ask questions to discover if we liked our school, were making friends, and enjoyed living in this place.

We did not feel so much at ease with the returned missionaries and the special Sunday speakers who came periodically to promote various causes—missions, peace, temperance, church colleges, prison reform, and so on. These men and women usually remained rather distant and enveloped in the atmosphere of their special concern. When Mother questioned them tactfully about their life in other lands or their particular areas of activities, hoping in this way to enlarge our horizons, few of them responded with enthusiasm. Still, over the years we did gain from such guests some appreciation of other cultures and ways of life.

It used to be customary in many Methodist churches to have a yearly series of revival meetings. My father's way of promoting Christianity was a quieter, steadier one, but since the more intense, dramatic method appealed to some of his parish, and since he definitely believed in the act of conversion, having experienced it himself, he conducted a series of evening meetings almost every winter. He did not call them revival meetings but Special Services, or A Week of Prayer. Neighboring ministers would come to help him in return for his helping them, and sometimes a regular evangelist would be employed. Naturally he would stay at our house.

One evangelist, I thought, used my father's study—even his desk —much too freely and made himself far too much at home in our house, even to asking the blessing at meals and conducting family prayers. I resented the parsonage atmosphere becoming strained with his talk about "battling for souls," and I avoided meeting him alone for fear he would question me about the state of my soul. Yet one day when I did encounter him I was annoyed and I think a little disappointed that he only remarked, "Little girl, what do you eat that makes you so plump?"

Often, especially in the summer, we had visits from our relatives. Among them were two girl cousins, more my brothers' ages than Helen's or mine. They were expected to abide by the household rules and regulations, and at least once Mother sent them to their room when they laughed too merrily on the Sabbath. But their visits were fun, with our having more picnics and excursions than usual and with more evenings made lively by music and games and young people coming in. They quite won my heart by coaxing Mother to let me go for a sail on the river with them and my brothers in a boat belonging to one of Walter's friends, who also was one of the party.

Nearly every year my mother's only sister and her small daughter would stay a few days with us on their way to a summer resort. This aunt was inclined to be critical, and Mother insisted that everything be done quite precisely during her visit. Though she always brought us very nice presents, she was not our favorite guest. My mother's brother, on the other hand, was a jolly fellow who became a real pal to my brothers. Once he and his wife spent a night with us following a European trip, and their account of their travels as well as the little gifts they brought us from distant places made a lasting impression on me.

Every year or two my mother's mother would arrive for a visit of three or four weeks. She seemed to me a very old lady, though she was not. She dressed in the customary widow's black, although her husband had been dead for several years, and wore a small black bonnet trimmed with a jet ornament and draped with a veil. She would help Mother with her eternal sewing, would sometimes go out with her to meetings or to make calls, and would sit in a rocking chair for hours on end crocheting or knitting. She went with us on our river picnics in the rowboat, but I think she did not particularly enjoy them.

During the summer a steamboat plied between our town and New London on certain days of the week, going on other days to Watch Hill, a popular seaside resort just over the Rhode Island line. Some generous executive had issued to ministers free passes which included their families. We counted an excursion on the

Martha a pleasant and inexpensive way of entertaining our summer guests.

Bound for Watch Hill for a day's outing, we would walk down to the river landing ladened with wraps, picnic basket, and bags holding bathing suits and towels. There we would board the *Martha* and enjoy an hour or two on the water. After we left the built-up area around the Watch Island pier we crossed a few grassy dunes and came to a quiet beach. Behind scraggly bushes we changed into our bathing suits and plunged into the sea or frolicked on the broad damp sand. Our lunch was enriched with Grandmother's gift of cheese and plums, and afterward we sat contentedly watching the never-ceasing waves, our backs against a protecting dune.

Once on our way back to the *Martha* Grandmother gave me a nickel to ride on the little merry-go-round that did an indifferent business not far from the landing. After thoroughly enjoying my ride I ran back to thank my grandmother. She looked at me disapprovingly and said, "I was disappointed in you, Edith. You sat astride your horse. No *lady* ever rides a horse that way. *Ladies* ride sidesaddle."

Once or twice a year an upstairs bedroom was turned into a sewing room and a seamstress came to spend several days with us, to help my mother get her wardrobe and Helen's and mine in shape for the coming season. Climbing the stairs we would hear the sound of women's voices, the click of scissors, and the busy hum of Mother's faithful old treadle sewing machine. The seamstress was treated like a guest, not a "helper," as were the widows or lone women who sometimes came to "help out" during the years after Mother felt she could get along without a steady "hired girl."

For long periods, usually when mother had no permanent help, an older half-sister of my father was a member of our household. Aunt Sarah was a New England spinster of forceful character. She adored her brother, was somewhat critical of his wife, frankly fond of the three boys, and indifferent to the two girls. She was also deaf as the proverbial post. "Auntie," who was an excellent cook, was glad to take over much of the responsibility of the kitchen and relieve Mother of the, to her, rather tiresome business of preparing meals. This enabled her to get out more frequently to make calls or go to church gatherings or to out-of-town meetings with Father.

Auntie was a striking figure of more than average height and weight, with slicked-back iron-gray hair, strong features, and spectacled blue-gray eyes. Her clear voice had a sort of nasal twang which was not disagreeable, and her sometimes rather salty comments were full of common sense. She seemed to understand most of what we said—partly, I believe, by reading our lips and even more by intelligent intuition. She was a great reader and, for a deaf person, read aloud amazingly well. This she loved to do because of the pleasure she saw it gave my father. We had many more read-aloud sessions in the evening when she was with us, and I remember her reading aloud the New England stories of Hawthorne, Harriet Beecher Stowe, and Sarah Orne Jewett.

Her devotion to the boys was evident to everyone. Mother said that when they were little she used to report their misdoings, then when Mother punished the miscreant by making him sit for an hour facing the corner Auntie would console him by slyly giving him a cookie and a kiss. As they grew older she delighted in making for them their favorite cookies or cakes and at Christmas presented them with the most awful ties which she had painstakingly made. They would admire them extravagantly, thank her profusely, and wear them only in her presence.

Aunt Sarah had been trained to be a teacher before she lost her hearing, and she was inordinately proud of every scholastic step ahead taken by the boys. She never missed one of their school commencements, from grammar school on through college. Often, because the others were tied up in one way or another, I was delegated to escort Auntie at various graduation functions—an arrangement neither she nor I really enjoyed.

At every graduation Auntie wore the stiff black taffeta dress reserved for church and special occasions. For Rob's college commencement she made herself a new black taffeta dress, heedless of Mother's suggestion that a summery material might be more appropriate. Class day dawned ghastly hot, and the slatted folding chairs, newly varnished for the outdoor event, felt the heat too. When the exercises were over we had to help pull Auntie loose from her chair. To our horror we saw that the varnish had left broad horizontal bands across the back of her dress, both above and below the waistline. We did not tell her this, not wanting to dim her pleasure in the afternoon. As she and I walked about the campus she was totally unconscious of people's half-concealed smiles but I was horribly embarrassed. Of course she discovered the disaster when she took off her dress at home and was very much upset. For days she and Mother tried to get out the stain but all efforts failed and eventually Mother helped her set in a new waist-back and skirt panel.

Though Mother had no real affection for Auntie or Auntie for her, they tolerated each other with reasonably good manners. Father, however, was "in the middle." He had to listen to Mother's complaints about his sister—that she went around with her petticoat showing, that she was extravagant in her cooking, that she stared at people, that she spoiled the boys. And he was very conscious of his sister's disapproval of Mother's ways—that she did not wait on him as a proper wife should do, that she let him help with household chores (definitely women's work), that she was over-fond of "gadding." But to Mother's credit we children were taught always to treat Auntie with respect and affection and never, never to make fun of her deafness—her "affliction." For every one of us Aunt Sarah was an important part of our growing up and a really memorable member of the parsonage family.

12. "In the Beginning God..."

This was the text of one of my father's sermons. It was also the guiding principle of his life. On it he based his ministry, his personal conduct and that of his family. "I should have liked to become a philosopher," he said once, "but I have given all that up. Here" (pointing to the Bible) "is my philosophy." And no one who knew him could doubt that with him God and the kingdom of God came first.

In all that my father did he had a staunch supporter in my mother. It was she who daily translated his ideals into reality in the home. Being good and doing good were held up constantly both by her and my father as the only right way of life, with the Bible as the only reliable guide.

Long before any of us children went to school each one learned the Lord's Prayer. At bedtime, kneeling with clasped hands beside his bed, each toddler lisped: "Now I lay me down to sleep." The twenty-third psalm was the first lengthy Bible passage to be memorized, followed by the hundredth and the hundred-and-twenty-first psalms and the Beatitudes—the "Blesseds," we called them. These were the passages most often recited in unison at Sunday morning family prayers, although we also knew many others. Every week at Sunday school the younger children received a small card on which a Bible picture was printed in color and beneath it an appropriate verse of Scripture known as a "golden text," which Mother saw was always memorized.

As soon as we reached reading age each of us received a sturdily bound King James Version of the Bible. Soon, at Mother's prodding, we learned the names of all its books in their order and were able to turn quickly to any one of them.

Being exposed very young to Bible readings, sermons, and religious talk beyond our comprehension led to some strange theological concepts. My first idea of death was connected with watching Father get into a horse-drawn hack, dressed in his Sunday Prince Albert frock coat and carrying his small black-leather ritual book. I was told that he was going to a funeral for someone who had died. Since there was no further explanation I thought death had something to do with a rather enviable carriage ride. Funeral homes had not yet come into being, and I learned that a black ribbon on someone's front door indicated that inside there was a dead person who, I judged from what I saw, was getting a lot of flowers. The funeral processions I occasionally saw seemed to me very elegant with the black-draped hearse, the black tassels hung on the horses' bridles, the profusion of flowers, and the long line of cabs and carriages. From Bible readings and hymns I visualized the dead person, who, I had been told, had gone to be with God in heaven, as standing in a vast open area facing a great golden throne. Somewhere on the way there he had acquired a white robe and wings and become an angel. I wondered if he and the other angels didn't ever get weary always standing, and I hoped that God would let them sit down sometimes.

When I was seven or eight the passage about the world's coming to an end troubled me exceedingly. Since this was to happen "in such an hour as ye think not," I reasoned that it could be prevented if somebody would keep his mind on it all the time. Without a word to anyone I took on the task and became a self-appointed watchman to stave off the Day of Judgment. I searched the skies at intervals for any forewarning signs of the catastrophe and tried to hold off the awful event by thinking about it as constantly as possible. But in a short time, as other pleasanter things crowded out my self-imposed duty, I abandoned the project.

I suppose I was especially conscious of death because my father was so often going to funerals. When I was twelve or so I was impressed by a conversation between him and a fellow minister as, standing before the campground book table, they discussed some book. Father was deploring the tendency to "pretty-up" death with fancy caskets, heaps of flowers, and gravesides lined with hemlock branches. "Give me in death a plain casket," he said, "and in life a faith strong enough to shout, 'Death, where is thy sting? Grave, where is thy victory?' " Although this did nothing to clarify my hazy ideas about death, it left a lifelong impression as to the depth of my father's religious beliefs.

In addition to the Bible, Father often gained inspiration for his sermons from the things around him. A towering three-limbed elm tree in the parsonage yard was the starting point for a sermon on the Trinity. Alas, a fierce gale blew down one of the limbs and left one of the remaining limbs leaning so dangerously over the parsonage roof that it was feared a high wind might bring it crashing down upon the house. Before it could be chopped down we had a heavy thunderstorm accompanied by a strong wind. Frightened and feeling our lives threatened, I ran upstairs, knelt by my bed, and implored God to stop the storm and spare our house. When the storm died down, leaving the two elm limbs still standing, I was sure that singlehanded I had saved our home. My faith in the power of prayer was enormously increased.

Soon after this I decided to test this power, depending on my father's words that God would hear anyone who earnestly prayed to him for forgiveness. I had whispered in school and had been seen doing it, but I brazenly denied the deed; then on the way home from school prayed earnestly to be forgiven for my lie. By the time I reached home I was convinced that this had been done and that I could dismiss the matter from my mind. But the next day I realized that something was wrong with my system, for I could see that I had forfeited the confidence and earned the disapproval of both my teacher and my schoolmates.

One morning a new grocery clerk came for our order and knocked at the side door instead of using the back one. It was during family prayers, and we were on our knees in the room the door opened on. Hearing the knock, I looked up and saw the young man. Overcome with embarrassment, I jumped up and ran into the next room. My father continued his prayer as if he had not heard the knock—as perhaps he had not. As soon as the prayer was over. Mother rose, went to the door, and calmly gave the boy her order. After he left she upbraided me for running out on what she admitted was a slightly awkward situation. Family prayers, she said, were nothing to be ashamed of, and if the young man was unfamiliar with them it was because they were not as commonly practiced as they should be. If this should ever happen again she hoped I would have strength of character enough to remain kneeling, as the rest of the family had done this time.

Part of my embarrassment, I decided, came from a desire for privacy in religious matters. Religion, I felt, was a private matter which should be free from even unintentional intrusion. In my mind I somehow connected this with my embarrassment when my father mentioned some member of our family or some family incident in a sermon. He rarely did this, but when he did, I squirmed in discomfort.

Often on Saturday mornings after my weekly dusting chore was done I would take a book and go to my father's study. There I would read quietly as he sat at his desk working on his Sunday sermon. Once in a while he would look up, name a book, and ask me if I thought I could find it for him. Usually I could, for I knew the titles of many of his books and the way they were arranged on the shelves. Although their insides might be unfamiliar to me, I was well acquainted with the back bindings of the sets of concordances, Bible commentaries, dictionaries, books of illustrations, and so on. Finding the desired volume pleased both him and me.

Sometimes Father would let me sit opposite him at his big desk and slit open the sides of long envelopes which had come in the mail so he could use the inside as scrap paper. Once I gleefully detached an uncanceled stamp and handed it to him. To my surprise he tore it in two. "That stamp has done its work," he said. "It would be dishonest to ask it to make a second trip."

When I was twelve the time had come for me to join the church, and my father called me into his study to talk about it. I knew that it was his duty as pastor to talk to people about religion, but I did not like it to happen to me. He was my father, and that was the way I wanted to keep him. Bracing myself against the tears that were near the surface, I answered his questions reluctantly. I must have seemed to him either unresponsive or obstinate or both. Yet, being a man of keen perceptions, he may have sensed, at least partially, my complicated feelings.

Being in the probation class, organized for the twelve-year-olds lined up to join the church, did not bother me so much. There was safety in numbers, and my father treated me just like the others—although, since the class met in his study, I felt a little like an unofficial hostess. He gave us each a small catechism, which he went over with us paragraph by paragraph, week after week. Then he would pray, and finally, as a sort of spiritual dessert, we took turns reading aloud *Pilgrim's Progress*.

At Christmas my father gave each member of the probation class a little book of Bible verses, one for every day of the year. On the flyleaf of my book, as of the others, was written: *From your pastor, J. N. Patterson*. This I deeply resented. Even though the book was given to me as a member of the probation class, he was still my father, not just *J. N. Patterson*. Let him be pastor to the others, but let him be a father to me!

The worst was yet to come. From now on, once or twice a year, Father called me into his study for spiritual talk and prayer. Those interviews always began something like this: "You must remember that I am your pastor as well as your father. I would be remiss in my pastoral duty if I did not counsel with you about your spiritual well-being." At these words my heart would harden. I could not accept the combination role of pastor and father. It was as if, as in the old enchantment tales, my father had been spirited away and a spiritual adviser put in his place. Feeling suddenly fatherless I rebelled and became callous to his words. The interview must have been difficult for him too, and I seemed to sense his relief as well as my own when it was over, after a lengthy prayer. For a few days our contacts were rather strained, then gradually we slipped back into our comfortable father-daughter relationship.

My father knew and dearly loved most of the hymns in the Methodist hymnal, which he called "a book of devotion." He chose the hymns to be sung in the church service with great care, selecting them to reinforce the message of his sermon. Because of this it was impossible for him to make his choice until he had finished or nearly finished preparing his sermon. This meant that the choir could not practice the hymns at their Thursday night rehearsal, but that was hardly necessary since they were usually familiar ones. Since it might be late Saturday morning or even Saturday afternoon or evening before the appropriate Sunday morning hymns were chosen, Father assumed the responsibility of posting their numbers on the board beside the chancel. Sometimes I would go to the church with him to help do this. Afterward he would mark the place for the Scripture lessons in the big pulpit Bible.

One Saturday, while waiting for him to finish, I carelessly sat on the communion rail and thoughtlessly bit into an apple I had carried in my pocket. Suddenly I heard my father's voice commanding me in sharp, unaccustomed anger: "Get off that rail! God could strike you dead for such desecration, even as he did Uzzah when he touched the ark of the covenant." I hastily obeyed, though almost petrified, both at the thought of being struck dead by an incensed God and at being spoken to so violently by my usually soft-spoken father, now turned into fiery man of God.

Although I accepted unquestioningly my father's dedication to his religion and his devotion to his ideals, I continued to experience a sense of desolation whenever his role as pastor seemed to override that of parent. Later I attributed my deep aversion to the Old Testament story often called "Abraham's Sacrifice of Issac" to that conflict. For, in addition to considering his child as a possession, this father was willing to put what he believed were the demands of his religion above those of his feelings as a parent.

It bothered my mother that Father encouraged comments and criticisms of his sermons at the family table. Father defended this permissiveness by saying, "It helps me discover my shortcomings. It also sharpens the children's wits and deepens their interest in spiritual matters." He would answer our questions frankly and try to explain things which seemed unclear. Sometimes he even conceded, "That's a good point," or "You've got something there."

Nothing derogatory of religious truths, as he saw them, was allowed, however, nor were these discussions ever permitted to become heated or emotional.

As the boys grew older they would introduce increasingly involved—and controversial—subjects. Once I remember Herbert or Rob mentioning a merchant's having installed a broad mirror at the back of his store. My father spoke up immediately. "That's wrong," he said. "It's a deception, intended to lead people to believe the store is twice its real size." But Walter disagreed. "It seems to me just good business," he said.

We were an undemonstrative family, not given to hugging or kissing except when someone was going on or returning from a journey of some distance or duration. But as a little girl I would often, just before getting into bed, run into my father's study in my flannel nightie, bend over his shoulder and kiss him goodnight. He would return the kiss fondly, never seeming to mind the interruption. My mother was more reticent about showing her affection, usually sending me up the stairs to bed—carrying the little tin lamp considered safer for my use than a glass one—with a crisp "Good night! Pleasant dreams!" When anyone was sick or going through a difficult time, however, she was less inclined to hide her feelings. "I wish I could do this for you, daughter," I remember her saying to me when, as a high-school girl I was about to have a tonsilectomy.

Mother played a very important part in my father's pastoral work. She kept in close touch with what was going on in the parish and she would tell him that this one was sick, that one was worried about her growing son, this couple was not getting on well together, or that high-school girl was believed to be "in trouble." The problems of the parish weighed on her as heavily as they did on my father, and neither of them ever flinched from a call for help. If the circumstances seemed to indicate a woman's presence rather than a man's, even the pastor's, she stood ready to go. But it was my father who called on the critically ill, prayed with the dying, stayed with the family during a member's operation, and was the first to reach a home after a tragedy had struck.

One morning while we were still at breakfast a police sergeant knocked at our door. He had come to tell of the drowning of a young man at a summer camp where he had been vacationing and to ask my father, as the young man's minister, to break the news

117

to the family. It was heartbreaking, for the drowned man was a fine fellow and the pride and support of his mother, a widow with two younger daughters. Father, his face white and drawn, asked for details and thanked the sergeant for the consideration of the police in not going directly to the family. He closeted himself in his study for a few moments, then prepared to go on his sad mission. The police sergeant went with him, planning to wait outside the house until Father had broken the news before going in to confirm it officially.

Father's task, we all knew, was one from which he shrank with all his tenderhearted being. Yet he did not falter; it was his duty and he knew his God would go with him. Afterward, since there was no one else to do it, Father made the long trip to the lakeside camp where the accident occurred, made arrangements for the removal of the body, selected the casket, and brought back to the family the dead man's personal effects. A day or two later he conducted the funeral.

People in trouble instinctively turned to Father, recognizing him as a "good man" and relying on his compassion, his understanding, and his deep trust in God. In one sense he had little knowledge of the world and its temptations, yet he had a sort of intuitive wisdom and his advice was likely to be sound. He advocated never running away from trouble. Stand firm; face the problem and with God's help overcome it, or, if need be, endure it.

My mother told me that in one community Father learned that one of his parishioners was in serious financial difficulty; it was thought that he had borrowed from funds entrusted to him. Unbidden, Father went to see the distraught man, who at first would not receive him, then relented. They paced up and down together, and the man told Father the whole story. My father prayed with him for forgiveness for the past and guidance for the future, then together they went to the man's superiors, whose money he had misused. They were persuaded by Father to map out a course which would eventually allow the man to make good the losses and restore his own and his associates' respect. To my father's joy that man proved worthy of their trust and of his confidence. In time, Mother told me, he even became a mainstay of the church and of the community.

Father did not try to answer people's persistent query: "Why?" When troubles and tragedies occurred he might quote Paul's words about seeing through a glass darkly that which would later be more fully understood. He never forgot that his help came from God, who made heaven and earth, and he regarded it as his mission and his privilege to help channel this strength to those who sorely needed it.

It would be impossible to estimate the number of people to whom my father brought comfort during the forty-four years of his Christian ministry. In his study was a small tin box which held no stocks and bonds but a few sentimental mementoes. Among them, Mother told me after his death, was a packet of letters from people in different parishes he had served—letters expressing appreciation for his kindness during a time of sorrow or thanking him for helping them over some rough spot in their lives, perhaps even changing the course of their lives.

"I never envy those who have more of this world's goods than I," Father said to me once. "The things I treasure money cannot buy. I am rich in the things of the kingdom—an easy conscience, the joy of having done some good, the privilege of working in the Lord's Vineyard." And, perhaps thinking of that packet of letters, he added, "As additional wealth, I have the gratitude of many men and women for some help I may have given them. What more could a man desire?"

13. Church Sociability

On Sundays the church sanctuary and the Sunday-school room were used exclusively for religious purposes. During the week the sanctuary stood idle but the Sunday-school room, which doubled as the church "parlor," was open for some kind of gathering almost every day and many evenings. These gatherings, except for the weekly evening prayer meeting and sometimes a second, sparsely attended evening service known as a class meeting, were not strictly religious in nature but were important in promoting church sociability.

The Ladies Aid Society made the most use of the church parlor. Made up of the women of the church it was without doubt the most important and active church organization. Not only did it contribute a substantial amount toward church expenses and toward home and foreign missions; it also took part in community projects and stood ready to help in local or distant emergencies.

Once a week the Ladies Aid met in the church parlor for an afternoon of work. Then the ladies rolled bandages for hospitals, made baby clothes and small dresses for orphanages, repaired used clothing donated for the barrels they sent periodically to missionaries for distribution to "the heathen," made articles to sell at the annual church fair, and worked on quilts and comforters to fill private orders. Each week two or three big quilting frames would be set up and a quilt-in-the-making stretched on each one. After a brief devotional service, experienced needlewomen would seat themselves around the quilting frames. Equipped with thimble, needle, scissors, and balls of floss, as well as with expertise born of long practice, they tied together the upper (patchwork) layer, the middle (cotton-batting) layer, and the bottom (calico or muslin) layer of the quilt-to-be. When all the patchwork squares within a foot or two in front of them had been tied they would adjust the frames to bring new areas within reach.

Anyone coming into the big room heard little sound from this part of the parlor but from across the room came the click of knitting needles, the hum of a sewing machine as someone stitched up the seams of a child's dress or the ties of an apron intended for the church fair, and the constant murmur of conversation. My mother tried always to go to these gatherings, not only to help and to "socialize" with the ladies but because she was sure to pick up more than one item she felt was important to pass on to her husband. Toward the close of the afternoon, as work was put aside, the pastor would often drop in to shake hands and say a few friendly words to each of the ladies.

Every month during the winter the ladies put on a church supper. These baked-bean suppers were popular not only with members of the church but with outsiders and were counted on to bring in considerable money for the upkeep of the church and parsonage. They were also cheerful social occasions. At the sewing afternoon the week before a bean supper, lists were made of those who would contribute baked beans, scalloped or mashed potatoes, cole slaw, brown bread, piccalilli or pickles, cake or pie. This was not difficult as the same women often donated the same dish each month.

The evening before the supper a few husbands gathered to set long boards over supporting sawhorses and spread over them the newsprint paper from the great roll contributed by a man in the newspaper business, then place chairs close together around the long tables. The next afternoon while women set out dishes, tin tableware, and heavy water glasses, the children who came with them folded paper napkins. As the food arrived, women set the beans and potatoes on the stove to keep hot, and others cut the cakes and pies.

Soon after six the people who had been gathering thronged to the long tables where they stood for the minister's brief blessing, then seated themselves with much scraping of chairs and noisy effort to avoid sawhorse legs. The hungry children, who must wait until after their elders were served, played outside or sat around the edge of the room miserably smelling the good food and hoping the grown-ups would leave enough for them. Strong-wristed women went around pouring the coffee while high-school girls, acting as waitresses, brought in heaping dishes of food. Young men tried to sit in the section waited on by their girl of the moment, knowing that their plates would never go empty. At last the sated adults rose, the tables were cleared and reset, and the second seating, for children and latecomers, was served. This done, the young waitresses gathered around the piano to sing and chat with the young men waiting for them, then drifted away in pairs or, failing this, took refuge in the kitchen to help with the cleaning-up process.

For variations on the usual bean supper there was a fall Harvest Supper, featuring chicken pie, and a Men's Supper, for which dishes were solicited and served by the men of the church. One year my father reported in his journal that at the Men's Supper everything went smoothly and a record sum of sixty dollars was cleared. He was on the solicitors' team and he wrote: "We had 13 chicken pies and 14 or 15 other pies, 2 Indian puddings, a large quantity of mashed potatoes and cabbage salad, 5 gallons of ice cream, rolls, butter, coffee, etc. No cake."

At the June out-of-door strawberry or ice-cream festivals, also put on by the Ladies Aid, people had their choice of strawberry shortcake, strawberries and cream, or homemade vanilla ice cream topped with strawberries—and a choice of homemade cake. These "festivals," like the winter church suppers, depended on the hard work of a handful of faithful women and besides contributing to the church financially, they added considerably to its spirit of fellowship and sociability.

So did the annual church fair, held in early December. Then aprons and other articles made at the weekly sewing sessions and contributed by individuals were put on sale. The fair, too, made much-needed money for the church and, even more than the suppers and festivals, brought together many church people and townspeople from other churches.

One social event traditionally sponsored by the Ladies Aid was a welcoming reception to the new minister and his family. For this the ladies went to much trouble to transform the rather bare-looking Sunday-school room by adding borrowed small rugs, floor lamps, palms and potted plants, and setting up a long table covered with someone's lace tablecloth; this held plates of small cakes and cookies and a punch bowl filled with a pleasant but innocuous pink drink.

This reception, well-intended as it was, was an ordeal for the newly arrived minister's family, tired from the strain of moving. Trousers needed pressing, cuff links turned up missing, shoes required blacking—and where was the polish? My sister's and my best dresses were full of wrinkles, our long hair had to be washed and then was unmanageable. Eventually, as always, Mother brought order out of chaos and we all were reasonably presentable when we lined up with church officials to shake hands, smile, and try to say a few pleasant words to everyone while well aware that we were being looked over with a critical eye. It was a relief when we could sit down, first to listen to welcoming speeches by other ministers of the town and church officials and to our father's brief reply, and then to enjoy the refreshments that were served.

Next to the Ladies Aid the Epworth League, the young people's society, was responsible for most occasions aimed at church sociability. During the winter this organization held a "social" at the church or in the parsonage each month. The program for this event was the responsibility of the organization's fourth vice president, in charge of "literary, cultural, and social" affairs. By some curious process my mother was never long in a place before she held that office. One way to fight card-playing and dancing, she felt, was to offer the young people of the church interesting entertainment and this, she was sure, she could do and could also make the programs uplifting and educational. By hard work and plenty of imagination she succeeded in making these monthly socials enjoyable events which were really looked forward to. She built programs around holidays and noted persons' birthdays, invited vacationers to distant places to tell of their travels and talented young people to play or sing, recite or read; she introduced get-acquainted games, simple quizzes, and funny little stunts. But how many Epworth Leaguers she kept from card-playing and dancing is anyone's guess!

The Sunday school sponsored few purely social events. Its chief function of course was to provide a weekly program of biblical and religious education for the children of the church. Children's Day in June featured special music, exercises, and recitations, and sometimes a drill—wand, scarf, or daisy—put on by a group of girls trained by my mother in weeks of painstaking practice. Rally Day, in September, was another special Sunday-school activity, again with special music and exercises, but not specifically a social event.

Twice a year, however—at its Christmas party and its mid-summer picnic—the Sunday school went all out in a purely social occasion. Some years, besides carol singing, piece speaking, and a decorated tree, the Christmas party included a well-padded, white-bearded, red-costumed Santa Claus whose task was to dispense from his big sack—with a *ho-ho-ho*—a small gift to each child. Other years the Sunday-school superintendent handed out red-net stocking-shaped bags, each of which had an orange in the toe and the leg part filled with candy and nuts.

One year the superintendent had the bright idea of creating a "missionary tree." Each child had been given a small brightly colored cloth bag into which to put a coin or two for the children at some faraway mission school. At the Christmas party the children themselves were to come forward and tie the bags to the lower branches of the Christmas tree. At the last moment the superintendent thought of asking each child to recite a Bible verse as he tied on his little bag, and he selected the minister's daughters to lead the performance.

As Helen stepped briskly to the front, where the tree stood, I said my verse over and over, proud of having thought of such an appropriate one. As I muttered softly "It is more blessed to give than to receive," to my horror I heard my sister saying the same words loudly and distinctly as she tied her bag to the tree. She returned to her seat beside me. I glared at her as I stumbled forward, trying desperately to think of another verse. Any verse would do, but I could not think of a single one; my mind was a complete blank; despite all my memorizing of Bible verses not one could I recall. I tied my bag to the tree in silence and, head down, went back to my chair. I felt I had let down my father and the whole family and was disgraced in the eyes of the church. A minister's daughter without a Bible verse—how shameful! And how, at that moment, I hated my sister!

The second Sunday-school social event, the annual picnic, came in early midsummer. It was really a church affair, not just for Sunday-school pupils but for all the church families. It might be held in a park on the outskirts of the town or perhaps a few miles farther away. Always it must be in a place with space for horseshoes, races, and a ball game. It might even have a little pond with rowboats to be hired. One year it was held in a park beside the Connecticut River, with motor launches plying back and forth to carry the picnickers. Another year a special trolley was chartered to take those without carriages or cars or bicycles to a large city park ten miles away.

The weather on Sunday-school picnic day was a matter of great concern, if not of prayer, but never to my recollection did the picnic have to be postponed because of rain. Long before noon men set up swings for the little children and quoit posts for the men wanting to throw horseshoes. Potato, bag, and three-legged races were organized and teams made up for the afternoon ball game. Each family brought its own lunch, but usually several families would eat together and there was plenty of sharing. The Sunday school always provided lemonade or pop, and sometimes it also furnished ice cream or juicy ripe watermelons. For once, eating was done without the formality of a ministerial blessing.

At these picnics there were always the "stay-putters" and the "go-rounders." There were plenty of these who made a point of strolling about from one group to another, getting acquainted, seeing that any who wished to take part in the different activities had a chance to do so, and that everyone—especially the children —had a good time.

Our whole family entered into all these social gatherings wholeheartedly, and Father knew he could count on the support of every member of his household in them as well as in the church's religious activities. Helen was equally willing to toss a ball at the picnic or to play hymns at the weekly prayer meeting. As long as the boys were at home, or later, whenever they came back for a visit, they too were willing to help out in any way. Often on a moment's notice they would play instrumental solos at either a religious or a social gathering. I contributed less, but at least I was always on hand!

Participating in the social as well as the religious life of the church made our tie with it both broader and happier. The hushed voices and sedate behavior our parents considered appropriate on the Sabbath were not required of us at these social affairs. Yet although then we could act more naturally, we were still expected to behave like ladies and gentlemen and not engage in any over-exuberant hilarity. For we must remember that as minister's children we were at all times Examples in both the church and the community.

III
Spreading Wings

14. "And Then There Was One"

Once again the time had come to move. After five years in a sleepy little town on the broad Connecticut we were to move to a larger, more industrial community on that same river some thirty or forty miles to the north. Since this appointment was not a double charge my father did not have the responsibility of a second church and could spend all his time and effort working in one community.

By now I was "the only chick left in the nest," as my mother liked to put it. Walter was married and establishing himself in the printing business. Herbert and Rob were through college; Herbert was teaching, Rob was in the hotel business in Washington, D. C., and Helen was attending the New England Conservatory of Music in Boston. I was finishing my first year in high school.

I missed the stir and fun of big family life, yet I found some advantages in being the only one of the younger generation at home. Parental discipline was more relaxed. "You didn't let *me* do that," Helen would sputter when vacationing at home. She was, I thought, over-critical of me, and our interests were still too far apart to make us good companions. I suppose I was unconsciously envious of her attractive appearance and easy social manners which made me feel awkward and incompetent. My parents, I thought, treated me more like an adult than she did. They included me in their conversations and often consulted me on family affairs as if my opinion really mattered. I reacted appreciatively to this, though sometimes it made me see myself as a person of some considerable importance. My father, sensing this, warned me to watch out lest I find myself "on the top of Fool's Hill." But I had heard him say the same thing to my brothers, years before, and so paid little attention. Going to a new place where people had not known me as a half-grown girl, I looked forward to being regarded as the minister's young-lady daughter.

It was agreed that my father should go alone to the new parish, leaving Mother and me to finish the last of the packing and also to allow time for our goods to get to their destination. Checking train schedules, the date and time were set when he was to meet us at the station in the new town. But when we arrived he was not there. We waited a short time, then took a cab to the parsonage address. Our repeated bell-ringing brought no answer, and it was soon evident that no one was inside. My sense of adventure, always keen when arriving in a new place, was fast oozing away and I was on the verge of tears. Not to be met, and then to be locked out of our new home—this was not adventure; it was disaster!

My mother did her best to cheer me up though she was downcast too. "I'm sure your father wouldn't have forgotten," she said. "He must have been called out on some emergency." And she suggested, "Why don't we take a look at the outside of the house while we're waiting?"

We left our suitcases on the front porch and started around the side of the large, pleasant-looking house. "See that wire coming in from the street?" Mother asked. "That means we'll have either a telephone or electric lights. What do you guess? Which would you rather have?"

In the parsonage we had left there had been neither. Thinking of the work of caring for kerosene lamps, I chose electricity. Besides, I said dismally, "What good would a telephone be to me in a place where I don't know anyone?"

"You'll soon have friends here," Mother predicted cheerfully.

At the back of the house we found a tree-shaded yard large enough for croquet and behind the trees a space for Father's garden. The absence of a small outside building made us pleasantly confident of indoor toilet facilities. We peered into the kitchen windows and tried the back door, which of course was locked, then returned to the front porch and sat ourselves miserably down on the steps. All the thrill of the new home had vanished.

Across the street we saw a door open and a woman emerge. She crossed the street toward us, smiling. Extending her hand she said, "You must be the new minister's family. There must have been some misunderstanding about your arrival or I'm sure you would have been met. Won't you come back with me and wait in my home?"

We accepted her offer gratefully, but as we started my father appeared. He was much upset at having reached the station just after we had left. It had taken him this length of time to walk back.

The friendly neighbor could see that we were eager to explore the inside of the parsonage together. She invited Mother to call on her for any help she could give, shook hands with Father, and left. "At least we seem to have one good neighbor," my mother remarked after she was out of hearing.

Father unlocked the door, and we stepped into our new home. In the parlor stood the piano, the only piece of our own furniture that had been set in place. The other downstairs rooms, which were crowded with boxes and barrels, looked large and light. Besides the double parlors there were a bedroom, dining room, and kitchen. Upstairs were a pleasant study (the front room), three good-sized bedrooms and a small one, besides the bathroom. "When we are settled, this will be a very nice home," Mother commented approvingly.

While we sat on boxes Father told us something about the town, the church, and the people. The town, while considerably bigger than the one we had left, was not overwhelming and we would soon feel at home in it. The church was two or three blocks away, the high school a bit farther. He had met the principal and liked him. The church people seemed friendly. The parsonage-committee ladies would be in the next day to see what they could do to help. They had brought in food, which he had put in the pantry and the icebox, where there was ice. Tonight we would take supper with a parishioner who lived nearby.

The meal in the home of the first of our church friends was pleasant if somewhat stiff. It was a relief to get back into our own place and to tumble into bed. I had chosen the corner bedroom; it overlooked the row of apple trees and the garden at the back, and at the side, beyond a hedge and lawn, the big house of our nearest neighbor. "Have a good night's sleep, daughter," Mother said. "We must be up and at work early tomorrow."

Father had engaged a husky young fellow for half a day and together the next morning they opened boxes, barrels, and trunks under Mother's direction. She put me to work upstairs lining bureau drawers with paper and carrying up and disposing of things that belonged in the study or bedrooms.

The wire we had seen coming in from the street proved to be connected to the telephone attached to the wall beside the front door. Mother made the first use of it to put in a grocery order. Father declared the telephone would be a "living nuisance," but before long he conceded its value and admitted he was willing to "eat his words."

At noon we stopped to eat a hasty lunch, and a little later the parsonage-committee ladies arrived. Mother thanked them for their offer of help but said she would have to "work her own way out of the present confusion." By dusk there was a slight semblance of order. The groceries had arrived and, tired out, we ate our evening meal at the kitchen table and got to bed early.

Until our first Sunday, Mother and I worked steadily unpacking and settling. We had met only the kind neighbor, the family who entertained us for supper, and the ladies of the parsonage committee. Now we must prepare to confront the whole congregation. Many eyes would be upon my mother and me as we walked down that center aisle for the first time. I did not feel at all like the grown-up young lady I had looked forward to appearing; my hands felt rough, my skin dusty, and my hair downright dirty. Somehow I managed to get my hair washed and a dress pressed.

Like most dreaded things, the reality was not as bad as the anticipation. Friendly people greeted Mother and me cordially as we entered the church and a pleasant usher escorted us to our pew. I wondered again why the minister's family pew must always be so far front! Looking up at my father I became more confident; it must be harder for him to face all these strange men and women, I thought, than for us to feel their eyes on our backs! The announcements included mention of the reception for the minister and his family. Here was something new to dread. It would be much worse than the first Sunday, I was sure, though probably not so bad as the first day at the new school—which was coming up the very next morning.

After Monday morning prayers I left my mother to struggle alone with the settling while I made my assault on the school. It was not so bad as I had feared. The teachers were pleasant and the new books and courses not too different from the old. My classmates, however, seemed to me worse than just indifferent. Not one of them made the slightest overture of friendship. Oversensitive, I had the feeling they were just watching and waiting for me to make some slip. Could it be that they were afraid I was a namby-pamby, goody-good, kill-joy kind of person because I was a preacher's kid—a "P.K."? I began to feel uncomfortable and homesick for my old school and companions, but I forced myself to wear a stiff little smile, determined not to let the situation get the better of me.

The second day went better than the first, and I began to realize that most of the indifference or worse was in my mind. Before the first week was over there had been a few exchanges of smiles, offers of pencils or books, and even a little conversation, and I began to feel less like a stranger. Within a month I had actually made a few friends—or at least acquaintances. There was little time for anything more, because in my out-of-school hours my mother needed my help at home.

The quicker we put the house in order, Mother insisted, the more at home we would feel. And so we worked like the proverbial beavers, with Father doing his full share. He moved furniture and hung pictures and mirrors. He set up his bookcases in the study and using some of the packing-box boards built himself a new one. Even with the parsonage shelves and his old personally owned knock-down ones there still was not enough space for

Father's books. When he started to put them on the shelves I was able to convince him that I knew pretty well the way he wanted them arranged, so he agreed to let me help. This was much more to my liking than washing dishes or spreading linen scarves on bureau tops.

The reception went off not too badly from my point of view. It was much like those I'd attended in other places—standing in line, listening to music and speeches, eating ice cream and cake. People paid me more attention, I decided complacently, than when I was just one of several children, the youngest of a big family, and they treated me at least halfway like the grown-up young lady I fancied myself to be. I was beginning to notice boys and rather missed some of those I had left behind. At the reception I was pleased to see several attractive looking boys of high-school age, a few of whom seemed to act a little as if they thought I might not be too uninteresting a person to get acquainted with.

When most of the settling, the first Sunday, the first day at school, and the reception were behind me I began to get adjusted to life in the new community. With my yen for exploration I would walk down different streets on my way home from school in an effort to discover the town. Sometimes, staring a little too hard at porches and windows I had the impression that I was not only looking but being looked at.

One day Mother asked me to bring home a box of crackers. On one of the streets I had found I had seen a new store where prices seemed to be lower than the ones we had been paying, so I bought the crackers there. This, it turned out, was the wrong thing to do. I should have gone to the store we were already using since it belonged to one of the church members. I protested. Weren't we trying to save money? Well, the box of crackers where I had gone was priced two cents lower than at the other store. This was unfortunate, Mother answered, but still we must give our trade to our own parishioner.

My parents left me pretty much to my own devices, although we did many things together. It was taken for granted that I would go to all the church services on Sunday, to the midweek prayer meeting, and to whatever else went on at the church in out-of-school hours.

Sunday, as always, was a big day for us. I soon began to sing in the choir and to teach a Sunday-school class of little girls. In the afternoon the Junior League meeting for the church children was held at the parsonage as Mother decided it was too much for her to make the fairly lengthy walk to the church and back in the afternoon as well as in the morning and again at night. I helped her with the Junior League girls and boys, playing the piano, not too well, for their songs. The high point of the meeting was the Bible story Mother told them each week, for she made it as dramatic as any of the series books they might be reading at home. At six-thirty she and I attended the Epworth League meeting at the church and then went on to the evening service, which finished our church day (and nearly finished us!).

Gradually life in the new town became familiar and natural to me. A new Saturday adventure I especially enjoyed was to go by myself on the trolley to the nearby city of Springfield. I would window-shop and wander through the big stores and then spend an hour in the reading room of the city library. Though not to be compared with it, I also found pleasure in investigating the contents of the dingy little town library housed upstairs in the town hall next to the high school. Often I preferred going there to spending the time fooling around with my schoolmates. My circle of girl friends was slowly expanding and I had a few casual acquaintances among the boys too. I still missed my friends in the old home, yet when I went back to pay a short visit on a former school pal I was surprised to feel almost like a stranger there.

At times I still missed tremendously being part of a big family. When my sister or my brothers came home for a holdiay or a weekend the place seemed to come to life and I realized how quiet our home was compared to earlier years. Yet being the only one of the "children" at home increased my self-confidence and my self-sufficiency. I was conscious of growing in many ways and of beginning really to achieve my ambition to be the young-lady daughter of the house.

15. Conflicts

One of the girls I met in high school gradually became my best friend. The church ladies were not pleased that she was not a Methodist or even a Presbyterian (the most popular denomination in town). Peggy went to the Episcopal church. Her family, however, was not one of the important "upper-class" Episcopal families of town. In fact, Peggy's father was an overseer in the carpet factory and his home was on a street of less than average prestige. Surely, the Methodist ladies thought, their minister and his wife would discourage this unfortunate friendship!

But neither of them did. Father took time to talk to Peggy one day when she came home from school with me and told me afterward, "Peggy seems like a very nice girl." And Mother repeated to me what he had said to her, "It would have been pleasant if Edith had found a congenial companion in our church, but since she didn't and she and Peggy seem really to like each other I see no reason why they shouldn't be together whenever they choose."

The days when the little town library wasn't open Peggy and I would often walk to her house or mine after school. In her mother's tidy kitchen we might make and eat fudge and at my house we might play croquet in the back yard, finger out some popular song on the piano, or sit on the front porch and talk about the boys at school. Peggy liked the boys and was popular with them—more so than I. She was a lively girl, always wanting to be doing things, and it was hard for her to understand my love of reading and books. Perhaps we became such good friends because we were so different. We didn't try to analyze the matter; we just knew we liked each other and enjoyed being together.

In high school Peggy was taking the commercial course while I was enrolled in the academic one. She was learning to type and I decided I'd like to be able to do this too. I requested permission to join the typing-class practice hour, which happened to coincide with my study-hall period, and rather to my surprise my request was granted. Pounding the typewriter keys was not so much fun as I had anticipated, but I kept at it and in this offhand way learned a skill which, I little realized then, was to serve me all my life. My parents considered my learning to type a passing whim—there was no typewriter in our home or any idea of investing in one.

While they did not object to this diversion, they did object—and very strenuously—when they heard I had taken part in a school play. The fact that it was only a small part and that the play was a sort of extension of the work of my English class, put on after school for students only, made no difference. Anything having to do with "play-acting" or the theater was anathema to my father. At church entertainments he would barely tolerate "skits," "tableaux," "impersonations," "a dialog," or "a dramatic presentation" where parts were read by two or three persons. Knowing this, I had not mentioned the play at home. Some of the church women with high-school-aged children spoke of it in my mother's hearing and one of them expressed surprise that the minister, who preached against the theater and acting, should have allowed his daughter to perform in the school play. As a result I was severely reprimanded both for acting in the play and for my silence about it. Never again should I do such a thing. Of course this quite took away the pleasure I had taken in being told by the English teacher that I had done my small part well.

When Father refused to let me go with my class to Hartford to see a noted Shakespearean actor appear in a Shakespeare tragedy I was both disappointed and angry. In vain I reminded him that we had read Lamb's *Tales from Shakespeare* aloud and that he had liked them. In vain I protested that a Shakespeare play was different from any other theater performance. Nor was he swayed by my tears or by what my teacher and classmates would think of me if I did not go. My father's answer continued to be a firm "No." Eventually I lived down my schoolmates' quizzical looks and got over my disappointment. But I continued to feel resentful.

The son of the Presbyterian minister was in my class at school, and although I did not especially like him I was flattered and pleased when he invited me to go with him to a movie in the town's one and only movie house. But I had to refuse, telling him that my parents wouldn't let me go because they disapproved of movies. *"All* movies?" he asked incredulously. As I nodded, the thought entered my mind for the first time that there must be a difference in movies; some must be better than others, or at least not so bad. Why did my parents believe that *all* movies must be bad? It must be, I decided, their feeling against acting—any kind of acting. I remembered my brother Walter's story about taking Father to see "The Birth of a Nation" when Father visited him in New York. "He walked out in the middle of it," Walter said, "and he said later, 'I see enough drama in real life without needing to see it play-acted.' "

Dancing, I had long known, was something else my parents considered sinful. I had heard Father mention sorrowfully a young lady who had not joined the church because she refused to give up dancing. "No good ever came of dancing," he declared firmly. What would my parents say, I wondered, if they knew that at some of the after-school fudge-making sessions at Peggy's and occasionally at other girls' houses I hopped around with them trying to learn a new dance step to the music of a phonograph record? Somehow I could not feel that this lively stepping about to music was the sin I had been taught it was. The theater, movies, dancing—were they all really wrong? I began to have some doubts about a few of my parents' convictions.

So far as religious matters went, I still did not question any of the beliefs I had been brought up in. Years of church and home training had thoroughly indoctrinated me, and I accepted what I had been taught without giving it much thought. The church continued to play an important part in my life. Besides five services on Sunday I went one evening a week to prayer meeting and another evening to a mission-study class. My parents had no cause to feel disturbed about my religious life, outwardly at any rate, but they could hardly fail to see the conflicts that were developing in the area of permissible and nonpermissible amusements. One taboo—that of card-playing—did not yet enter the picture because none of my close friends happened to be much interested in this diversion.

It bothered me that I did not have as many high-school boys calling on me as most of my girl friends did. I could understand why. They did not feel at ease in my strictly supervised parsonage home, and they knew that I could not go with them to the movies or to any party where there might be dancing. Sometimes on a hot summer evening one of the boys would come over and we would sit together on our front-porch swing. This was not a very private place, in spite of the profusion of vines climbing the trellis. People came and went along the sidewalk only a few yards away and once in a while someone would come in or go out of our front door. Neither Mother nor Father made any objection to these informal evening calls, or to boys bringing me home from church and staying a while, or to my taking Saturday-afternoon walks with boys—even those who did not attend our church—along the riverbank paths.

Quite a different matter was an invitation I received to go on an evening double date to Springfield to see a highly recommended play. When I spoke to my mother about the invitation I called it a "performance" and carefully avoided the word "theater," but I am sure she knew the truth. She could see that this was an important occasion for me—my first really grown-up experience. She wavered and said that she would have to speak to my father about it. I insisted that there was nothing wrong about the plan and that I thought I was old enough now to make up my own mind about such things. I am sure that when she talked it over with Father she too avoided using the words "play" and "theater." I am sure too that she did not feel quite easy about the matter in her own conscience when she told me that they had agreed to leave the decision to me; they would regret my going but they would not prohibit it and I must understand it would be without their approval. I went and enjoyed my first real theater experience—to a point. The knowledge of my parents' disapproval rather took the edge off my pleasure.

The real showdown with my parents came over the matter of the high-school dance. Every year or two a carefully chaperoned dance was held in a rented hall, with a rented orchestra, for the benefit of some high-school project. All the students were urged to attend, and no effort was spared to make this a very nice and enjoyable affair. For weeks the big topic of conversation among the girls was who would take whom to the dance. I knew no one would ask me, since my father's disapproval of dancing was well known. Then I heard several girls say that they were going by themselves in order to have their pick of the unattached boys there rather than being stuck with one partner, and it occurred to me that perhaps I could go that way too. Never having been to a dance I visualized it as a big, gay party—with dancing, to be sure, but with a lot of fun for everyone.

That was the way I presented the affair to my parents. I called it a "reception," and said, rather exaggeratedly, that all high-school students were expected to attend and that not to go would be considered being disloyal to the school. Neither of my parents had any more idea than I did of what such a dance was like. Their scanty knowledge of dances and dancing was based on strongly biased personal accounts of church members who had earlier sown their wild oats and on anti-dancing articles in church papers. My father persisted in speaking of the occasion as I had done—as a reception. Both he and my mother respected the high-school principal and liked what they knew of the small staff of teachers. They wanted me to enjoy my school life and to participate in its activities. And yet—

For days they refused to give me a definite answer. I knew they were discussing the matter and praying about it. At last my mother spoke to me. "I'm sure you could not really expect your father to condone his daughter's going to this affair when he feels so strongly that dancing is wrong and even preaches against it in the pulpit. But this reception seems to be an important school event and we both know how much you want to go to it. And so"—drawing a deep breath—"we have decided on a compromise. You may go if you will give us your word that you will not dance."

I was innocent enough to be pleased. On the big night I put on my best dress and walked alone to the hall. Leaving my wrap in the cloakroom I presented my ticket, received a little dance card, and went into the big hall. An orchestra was playing and my schoolmates were dancing. At one side of the dance floor I saw several of my teachers sitting in a group. I went over and spoke to them, which I thought was probably the correct thing to do, and when they invited me to sit down with them I did this, not knowing what else to do. After a few minutes I left and went to sit on the side lines beside some girls. I watched my friends on the floor and thought bitterly that they were having too good a time to pay any attention to me. A few boys timidly approached and asked me for a dance and when I shook my head they went on to other girls. My little dance card must, I knew, remain blank.

During a pause in the music two of my girl friends—one of them Peggy—came over to me. Beckoning their escorts, they insisted that we all go back stage where, they said, I could dance without being seen. Surely, since I would not be on the dance floor and not in sight, this would not be breaking my promise. I listened and went with them. When the music started again I awkwardly danced a few measures with the accomodating escorts, but my lack of practice, my first experience of dancing with a boy, and my guilty conscience prevented this from being at all satisfactory. The back-stage party soon broke up, my friends went back to the dance floor, and I to my seat along the wall.

The evening was becoming one prolonged agony. For another hour or so I brazened it out, again and again asking myself why I had ever come but unwilling to admit defeat by leaving too early. At last, when I thought no one was noticing, I crept out, got my wrap, and headed for home—alone. When I reached the residential street the parsonage was on I crossed to the other side where there were fewer street lights, where trees overhung the sidewalk, and where the houses were set farther back in their lawns. I prayed that I would not meet anyone I knew and that no neighbors would be sitting on their porches where they could see me. The house was quiet; my parents had gone to bed. I tiptoed up the stairs, took off my fine apparel, and got into bed where I cried myself to sleep.

The next morning I put on a brave face. It had been a fine party, I lied, and I had had a wonderful time. But for weeks I hated myself for having gone to the dance and my parents for having let me go, bound by the promise not to dance. I imagined that everyone at school, including my teachers, eyed me pityingly and that even Peggy was not quite so friendly. Gradually this feeling wore off and things got back to normal.

In the fall I went to a Halloween party at a country club with a nice-looking lad who came to get me bringing a giant chrysanthemum. It was far too large to wear and a nuisance to carry, but I took it along anyway; it was precious because it was my first such gift. There was square dancing at the party, in which I awkwardly took part, telling myself that this was not really dancing—at least not the kind my parents objected to—and that not to join in would make me conspicuous and embarrass my escort.

That winter I gained a little more understanding of my parents' feeling about the theater when, quite unexpectedly, I was invited to go on a sleigh-ride party with a rather grown-up escort and a group of young people whom I considered quite sophisticated. It was a jolly ride to Springfield, where we attended a vaudeville show—my first. I tried to appear nonchalant but was really uncomfortable and uneasy. I'd never seen such abbreviated costumes, much of the dancing seemed to me vulgar, and the jokes impossibly crude—and partly beyond my comprehension. It flashed into my mind that if this were the sort of thing my parents associated with the words "theater" and "dancing," their outlook was not entirely unreasonable. But, I argued with myself, not all theater—in fact, probably very little of it—was like this, and they should realize that fact.

Clearly I was beginning to spread my wings and to see things through my own eyes rather than those of my parents. At the same time I was gaining a degree of understanding—though not of sympathy—with their viewpoints and losing a little of my bitterness toward their outlook. These years, I began to see, were difficult ones for my parents as well as for me. I noticed that it

troubled them when they gave ground on matters about which they felt strongly, and I suspected they worried for fear in doing so they were being unfaithful to their beliefs. I knew they prayed daily for guidance in my upbringing—and it made me uncomfortable.

To my parents' credit more than to mine our life together was for the most part harmonious and pleasant. The church and home routine went on as usual, in spite of our frequently differing points of view in what, I was coming to realize, were not the most essential matters in life. During these high-school years I was learning a lot of things in addition to what I was taught in school. Life was not, I decided, an altogether black-and-white affair, and neither books nor my parents had all the answers, though for years they continued to be the two greatest influences in my life.

16. The Donation Party

Donation parties, once a common substitute for a pastor's salary, were a thing of the past by my time, at least in our part of the country. Some of the very old-timers in the parish could perhaps remember the days when farmers would drive in from the country to leave at the preacher's door a butchered pig or a load of potatoes in lieu of making cash contributions to the church. Or they might have heard of rural parishioners getting together to present their practical gifts jointly in a joyous occasion known as a donation party. "Cash money" was scarce with them then, even scarcer than in the days of my father's ministry when, though ministers were thought of as salaried professional men, small churches still found it hard to pay them promptly or regularly.

In our family when a church member from an outlying farm brought us a dozen ears of corn or a basket of melons we regarded it as a kind and generous gesture bearing no relation to the man's financial arrangements with the church. We felt the same way about the occasional gift of a jar or two of jelly or canned fruit some woman parishioner presented us during the canning season. Equipment for the house, such as a carpet sweeper or a door mat, we thought of as part of the furnished-parsonage deal.

But when I was in high school an energetic, well-meaning woman in our church, having read of the old-time custom of donation parties, conceived the idea of getting up one as a novel sort of surprise party. This seemed to her an original way of using a traditional pattern to show the minister and his wife how much their congregation thought of them.

Some of my friends whispered to me word of the coming surprise party at the parsonage and of course I passed the word on to Mother. She urged me to try to find out the date. "But don't breathe a word of it to your father," she cautioned. "At least he can be really surprised, and you and I will have to act that way."

With a little difficulty I was able to pin down the date. "We must see to it that the whole house is sparkling," Mother said. "At times like this they always wander all over." And so she and I cleaned and "tidied" every room, polished furniture and silverware, and cleaned and filled all the lamps. We even got down our best china for, Mother predicted, "They'll be sure to bring refreshments."

On the appointed evening Mother saw to it that supper was finished early and Father hurried off to the study. But when I started upstairs to change my school dress for something better she stopped me. "We must look neat (one of her favorite words) but not dressed so that anyone would suspect us of knowing about the party. I'll not light the parlor lamp either; we can do that after they come."

My mother answered the ring at the front door and welcomed the two or three women who stood there, their arms full of packages. Almost without leave they made their way through the house to the kitchen where they dropped their loads on the table. They had come for a little visit, they said, and thought it might be pleasant later on to have a cup of coffee and a bite of cake—

145

which accounted for their packages. They hoped this was all right. They also hoped the minister was home and that later they might visit with him too.

Methodist minister's wife or no, my mother was a born actress. She rose to the occasion, expressing her pleasure at the unexpected visit and at their thoughtfulness in bringing refreshments. And she assured them that the minister was in his study. By the time she lighted the parlor and other downstairs lamps more people, both men and women, had arrived. Like the ladies who preceded them, they were loaded with bundles, most of which found their way to the kitchen. While leaving their wraps in the downstairs bedroom this second group informed Mother that this was really a little surprise party. Better not alert the parson till the rest had arrived, they suggested. They would talk softly so that he would not suspect anything from his upstairs study.

When both the parlor and the sitting room which opened out of it were full of people the time had come, they decided, to include my father in the festivities. Mother went to the foot of the stairs and called up: "John, please come down. There are a few callers here who want to see you."

We could hear him fumbling around in the study as he closed his books and straightened his coat and tie before starting downstairs. As he neared the bottom step, "Surprise!" the "callers" shouted in the best approved style. And Father really *was* surprised. His astonishment delighted the parishioners who congratulated one another on "putting one over on the parson."

Father went around shaking hands with everyone, exchanging pleasantries, and inquiring for absent and ailing members of families incompletely represented. As more men and women arrived they found places in the dining room or on the parlor or sitting-room floor. Two young ladies who "just happened" to bring along some music were asked to entertain with piano and vocal solos. Then someone called for a recitation from Father. Without hesitation he gave "Darius Green and His Flying Machine" and for an encore "The Tale of the Nancy Belle." Next someone suggested a guessing game. This provided fun for everyone and a chance to act funny or clever or coy without too much taxing of the brain.

Then came the high point of the evening. The woman who had instigated the party made my father and mother and me stand,

and the friendly men and women—singly or in pairs or small family groups—came up and presented us with gifts. This turn of events took not only my father but my mother and me completely by surprise. My slyly gained knowledge of the party had not included information of anything of this sort.

When the gifts filled our arms and overflowed into a nearby chair the woman who had started it all made a little speech. She had read, she said, of donation parties which happened long ago and had conceived the idea of recreating one today. She was sure this was the first time anyone present had attended such an event and she hoped everyone was enjoying it. Her speech over, she buzzed about happily receiving compliments on her ingenuity and initiative. Now the occasion was no longer a simple surprise party; it had become a unique, noteworthy Donation Party.

For me, it had become a nightmare. While my mother and father graciously accepted place mats and towels, embroidered doilies and handmade aprons, peach preserves and home-canned pears, boxes of candles, pencils, and soap, I received the handkerchiefs, notepaper, and candy handed me with a forced smile and struggled to fight back tears. Luckily more attention was paid to my parents than to me, and no one, I am sure, suspected that with each gift my pride was wounded and my sense of independence shaken. Only a minister's family, I was thinking, would be expected to show pleasure as they endured the disgraceful affront of receiving charity in the guise of "donations." I was overcome with shame. Let them increase my father's salary, I thought bitterly, not donate provisions and household articles!

After the bestowal of gifts and the instigator's little speech the chairman of the official board stepped forward. He was a man who dearly loved to make a speech and would do so at every possible opportunity. Now he voiced the sentiment of all, he said, in being indebted to the originator and promotor of this unusual party for this effective way of showing the pastor and his family their congregation's regard for them. And as an extra memento he was entrusted with something from all here this happy evening and from others who could not be present—a little something for the parson to slip into his pocket. With a flourish the speaker produced a leather wallet which he presented to my father.

Father was truly touched. He had not fully realized the deep affection in which he was held by the people of his parish. Opening the wallet—by far the nicest he had ever had—he found it bulging with dollar bills and coins—$17.50, according to the entry he made in his journal the following morning. It was a real tribute, for these were not wealthy people. He expressed his appreciation briefly and sincerely.

For me, this gift of a purse only added fuel to the fire. So they were giving us money too! What did they think we were—paupers who had to accept handouts?

Somehow I lived through the rest of the evening, struggling to smile and be good-mannered—and to keep my inner thoughts from showing. The fragrance of coffee coming from the kitchen and the sight of the chocolate and angel food cakes restored my spirits a little. In a happy, relaxed, self-satisfied (I imagined) atmosphere the self-invited guests drank coffee and ate several varieties of cake. At length, some of the ladies having helped clear up the kitchen, they left after—they all said—a most enjoyable evening.

When the last one had gone, to my parents' astonishment I burst into tears, then broke into a tirade. I denounced the whole lot of them as crude, unfeeling, insensitive people. I knew we were poor, I wailed, but did everyone think we were so poor that we needed to be given soap and towels and jelly and jam? How could I ever explain this to my high-school friends? Oh, it was intolerable!

Both Mother and Father were aghast at my outbreak. It took them a while to understand my feelings and longer to calm me down. Why, they asked, couldn't I see it as they did—as a warm-hearted, generous gesture. They saw nothing at all demeaning about it. They tried to convince me that my attitude was entirely wrong, but they did not succeed. I even threatened to stay home from school the next day to avoid the humiliation of confronting my schoolmates—an idea they vetoed with absolute finality.

To my surprise the next day in school was like any other. No one paid any special attention to me or made any snide remarks or looked pityingly at me as I had been so certain they would do. In fact, the few girls whose parents had been at the party mentioned it in what seemed to be a rather envious way.

But that evening the heaviest blow fell. The Springfield daily paper carried a small section devoted to the doings of our town and glancing through it that night my eye fell on a column headed "Donation Party." Below was a full account of the affair, stating that at the Methodist parsonage the previous night the old-time custom of donation parties had been revived most successfully, with the minister's family receiving generous donations of "food, clothing, and money."

I raged. Yes, I admitted, there had been food, though most of it had been eaten by the people who brought it. And yes, there was clothing—an apron for Mother, a tie for Father, and a scarf for me. And no one could deny there was money for Father. Sobbing now, I visualized the whole town as gloating over our shame. Today, I had to admit, had not been bad at school, but this was probably because not many knew about the shameful affair. Now everyone would know and tomorrow would be hideous. I'd certainly not wear the made-over dress Mother had just finished for me; if I did, everyone would think it was some of the "clothing" donated at the party.

My parents wisely let me rage on until I ran down. They did not labor the matter with me again but counted on time to heal my wound—real or imaginary. Once more anticipation was worse than realization and no unpleasantness occurred at school either the following or any other day.

The next morning at prayers Father chanced to read the Bible passage containing Jesus' words: "The poor ye shall always have with you." I snorted and began to relive my grievances and get myself into an unpleasant mood. After we rose, following the prayer, I began to argue with Father. Why did Jesus predict there would always be poverty in the world? I asked him. Did there need to be?

Instead of answering me directly Father interpreted my questions as biblical criticism and began to upbraid me. In an effort to calm things down, Mother interrupted and told Father she needed a check that morning and would he please write it out immediately, before he went up to the study. Father sat down at her desk in the corner of the room, picked up a pen, and opened the checkbook. In a moment we heard him chortling. Displaying the check he had just written he pointed to his signature: *J. N. Poverty*. None of us could help laughing, and the situation lost its tenseness.

Little by little, as other things absorbed my time and attention, I forgot about the donation party. My indignant resentment died down and my sense of injury wore off. I could even begin again to feel kindly toward the people of our church—with the exception of the woman who thought it all up; that would take a while longer. After a few weeks I had regained my sense of proportion and could begin to see the ridiculousness of my attitude. Yet the experience had left a sore spot within me which for years hurt a little whenever I read about that old-time custom, the donation party.

17. "I Do!"

One of the pleasures in my being accepted as an adult was that of acting as a witness to marriages performed by my father. During my high-school years I probably witnessed more weddings than most people see in a lifetime. And "witnessed" is the correct word.

The reason lay in the difference between Massachusetts and Connecticut marriage laws. In Massachusetts, persons intending to marry must secure a license five days before the marriage, while at that time there was no such requirement in Connecticut. Consequently Massachusetts couples seized with a sudden matrimonial impulse often traveled by train or trolley across the state border to the closest Connecticut town—in one of which my father was a minister. At the town hall they purchased a license and inquired the way to the nearest preacher. Since the Methodist parsonage was on the same street as the town hall just an easy walk away, it was where the town clerk's assistant, a gentle spinster lady, usually directed them. Sometimes she even telephoned to announce: "A wedding is on the way."

It was my father's practice to leave word when he went out where he planned to be, so that if necessary he could be quickly located. If he told Mother that he was going to make calls in a certain neighborhood she would not hesitate to telephone a parishioner in that neighborhood, if the need arose, and ask to have him tracked down. As a rule he would be riding his bicycle and so could be spotted easily and could get home in short order.

Two witnesses were required by law, and for these unscheduled weddings they were usually my mother and me. I found it exciting to be introduced to the bride and groom and to be a part of this romantic event. Nothing in the formalities and informalities preceding, during, or following the ceremony was lost on me.

After a few moments of casual talk aimed at putting the couple at ease, Father would ask to see the license. While he was examining it in his study Mother and I would continue the conversation. In a few minutes Father, having found everything in order, would reappear, wearing his Prince Albert coat and carrying his ritual book. He would inquire of the bride and bridegroom what their Christian names were, if there were one ring or two, and whether they preferred the full marriage ceremony or a shorter form. He would instruct them on the responses they should make and tell them what to do with the ring or rings. Mother and I noticed that the bride often knew these things while the groom rarely did, and that of the two it was generally he who appeared the more nervous and ill at ease.

When the couple took their places facing my father, my mother and I would sit quietly at one side of the parlor. Although Father always opened his book to the wedding service I doubt if his eyes really saw the words, he knew them so well. And so, before long, did I. I felt the same surge of pride in my father as he performed a wedding ceremony as I did when he was in the pulpit. By his voice and bearing he made the marriage service take on such significance that its beauty and solemnity must have impressed even the flightiest of couples.

At the conclusion of the ceremony I watched with interest as the bridegroom kissed the bride. Sometimes he did this awkwardly, sometimes with embarrassment, and sometimes with passion. After shaking hands with the couple and offering them his good wishes Father would retire to the study to fill out the certificate which he would give them. This was not a legal document but a keepsake signed by the minister and witnesses and usually treasured for life by the couple.

My father kept on hand a supply of two types of wedding certificates, both of which he ordered at his own expense from a church supply house. The one for the rank and file of marriages was a single sheet of parchment embellished with clasped hands and a dove and suitable for framing. The other, for the "fancier" weddings, was a rather elaborate brochure; its pages, laced together with white cord ending in tassels, contained spaces for bridal pictures, witnesses' signatures, and appropriate remarks. Whichever kind Father brought down from the study indicated to Mother and me the size of the fee he thought he would receive from the bridegroom. This was of considerable interest to us, for by tradition wedding fees went to the minister's wife and in our family she generously used them for something special for us all. They might provide a few extra days of vacation or a better vacation cottage or something we all wanted for the house.

The moment when we saw the groom put his hand into his pocket was a tense one. Would he bring out a sealed envelope containing a five- or a ten-dollar bill, thus justifying Father's choice of the brochure certificate? Or would he awkwardly hand the minister two or three single bills? It was not unusual for the groom to ask, "What is the charge?" To this Father would reply, "There is no set fee," and sometimes with a twinkle in his eyes he would add, "Pay whatever you think it is worth." This touch of humor, however, was more likely to puzzle than to amuse the bridegroom. For these unscheduled parsonage marriages two dollars was a more or less normal fee, but a five-dollar bill was not at all unusual—or, unfortunately, a one-dollar bill. Very rarely it was ten dollars.

Father told some amusing stories about marriage fees in his early days as a minister. One young farmer offered him "a couple bushels of potatoes in the fall or a dollar now." Father said he thought it wiser to choose the dollar in the hand than the potatoes still in the ground. To another bridegroom who said he "could do better by the parson later," Father suggested he'd "better do what he could now and have it off his mind." And mother recalled the young tradesman who evidently had not included a minister's fee in his calculations. When the idea suddenly occurred to him immediately after the ceremony Mother said she watched with amusement as he scrambled through his pockets. He gathered up a few quarters here, a few dimes there, and a few nickels elsewhere, and finally counted out, entirely in small coins, one dollar and eighty-five cents, which he presented to the minister.

One day a nice-appearing lad drove in from a rural neighborhood to engage Father's services for a wedding at his bride's home two weeks later. He also asked Father to conduct a rehearsal so that everything would go off flawlessly. Both families, my father deduced, were well-to-do farming people. Naturally Mother and I could not help letting our thoughts jump ahead to the good-sized fee this indicated! On the wedding day Father, dressed in his best Prince Albert and bearing the brochure-type certificate, rode out in the buggy which had been sent for him. When he returned he handed Mother a small envelope. Her face lighted with pleasure as she felt a coin inside; gold pieces were rare as wedding fees—or any other way. She tore open the envelope and we saw a strange expression spread over her face. Unbelievingly she held up—a fifty-cent piece. For a moment there was stunned silence, then we all broke into laughter. What a let-down!

For the parsonage marriages Father always completed filling out the license, which the couple had brought from the town hall, just as soon as they left. It had to be returned to the town hall within a specified number of days, and Father often entrusted me with doing this since the town hall was next to the high school. In this way the town clerk's assistant who handled the licenses and I became friends—a fact which I liked to think played a little part in her sending future couples our way.

Many of these parsonage weddings were quickly forgotten. Others were long remembered, usually by reason of some dramatic quality or humorous happening.

One bridegroom, a small, neatly dressed, middle-aged man, wore a white flower in his lapel and a conspicuous white bandage on his right thumb. He had cut it badly the day before, he said, and it was evident that it hurt him for he circled it protectively with his left hand and kept it pointed upward. Every now and then, surprised by a sudden spasm of pain, he would jerk the bandaged thumb several inches into the air, a look at consternation would spread over his face, and he would whistle "Gosh!" softly but audibly through his teeth. This struck me as terribly funny and when, in the middle of the ceremony, I saw the bandaged thumb bob suddenly upward and heard the bridegroom unmistakably whistle "Gosh!" it was hard for me not to laugh. It must have struck my father too as funny, for he hesitated a second or two— to steady his voice, I was sure—before going on with the ceremony.

One bride and groom annoyed yet amused me by chewing gum (something I was not allowed to do) throughout the entire marriage service. They chewed vigorously and with apparent relish. They even seemed to keep step, as it were, with each other, losing the beat only when it was necessary for one or the other to pause to say "I will" or "I do."

We remembered one bridegroom because of his coat. It was a cutaway, about three sizes too small for him. Mother and I surmised later that he had borrowed it for the occasion, thinking it to be the correct wedding-day apparel. To avoid seemingly inevitable disaster the poor man moved very little and when he did, his motions resembled those of a wooden soldier. The bride was simply and appropriately dressed, and we thought she must have been as relieved as we were when they were able to leave the parsonage with the bridegroom's coat still intact.

Another time it was not the bridegroom's but the best man's costume that caught our eye. The friend whom the shyly-spoken bride and groom had brought along to stand up with them was resplendent in checkered waistcoat and broad purple tie agleam with diamond stickpin. It was he who acted as spokesman for the bridegroom and who did most of the talking both before and after the ceremony. During the service, when my father said, "Let us pray," I saw him start to drop to his knees, then—seeing that no one else was doing this—recover himself and regain an upright position with amazing alacrity. But he surprised us most when at the end of the ceremony he rushed in between the newly-weds and gave the bride a resounding smack before the quiet bridegroom had a chance to kiss his bride.

As the three of them left the best man boasted, "Shouldn't wonder if you'll be seeing me again before long. May be getting married myself. Don't know just when. Haven't asked her yet." Sure enough, a month or two later he returned, more quietly dressed as bridegroom than as best man. With him was a tall, glum girl who never smiled and who spoke only when spoken to. She had little need for speech; her husband talked enough for both!

In contrast to this man was a bridegroom who was painfully silent. He barely answered Father's conversational questions and ventured no remarks at all on his own. But when in the ceremony my father put to him the question: "Wilt thou have this woman to be thy wedded wife?" the quiet man startled us almost out of our skins by fairly shouting: "I CERTAINLY WILL!"

One unannounced couple seemed overly nervous. They requested my father to marry them as quickly as possible as they wished to catch a certain train. This Father did by using a short form of the ceremony, and within a few moments the two were married and on their way, the signed certificate in their hands. Father was still in the study filling out the license when there was a furious ringing of the doorbell. I opened the door to a heavy-set man out of breath and very obviously out of sorts. His loud demand to see the minister brought Father down the stairs. Shaking his fist at him the man shouted, "You married them! I know you married them! I tracked them here. What right did you have to marry my daughter to that good-for-nothing?"

Father invited the enraged man into the parlor and tried to talk to him quietly. The man would not listen but kept on ranting. When he threatened to have the law on my father "minister or no minister," Father politely but firmly escorted him to the door. "Threats will get you nowhere," he said quietly. "The young people's license was in order and they were clearly of legal age. Now" —closing the door on the irate man—"I'd suggest you go home and try to calm down."

Another time the short service was used to accomodate a dance team appearing in a "four-a-day" vaudeville house in Springfield. They had figured out a way to be married and to miss only one performance. They could catch a southbound train after they had done their act in the second show, get down to Connecticut and be married and get back to Springfield by trolley just in time to go on in their usual place in the fourth performance. To test the plan and to save time on their wedding day the groom made the trip down the day before, bought the license at the town hall, and —at the town clerk's assistant's suggestion—telephoned my father to engage his services for early the following evening.

To the couple's dismay the next day the southbound train was late. This shortened their time, but my father was waiting for them, as were my mother and I. Though unsympathetic with their profession, Father was understanding of the couple's race with time and he married them with the utmost dispatch. After signing the certificate as witness, I rushed to an upstairs window where I could see the light of the northbound trolley as it came in sight half a mile away. When I cried, "There it comes!" the pair grasped their certificate, bade a hasty goodby, and made a dash for the corner stop where they boarded the trolley. With luck they would be back on time for their last appearance of the day—their first as a married team.

Superstition, I learned, played a part in some marriages. One bridegroom fingered a lucky piece throughout the ceremony. Another asked my father to use his nickname in the service instead of his baptized name explaining, "The moniker my parents stuck on me has brought me nothing but bad luck." A few brides chose their wedding day by working out lucky number combinations and many set it to coincide with a birthday, a holiday, Valentine's Day, or a favorite anniversary. There was rarely a wedding on a Friday or on the thirteenth. One mother refused to witness her daughter's marriage, believing this would bring bad luck, but she agreed to sit in the adjoining room where she could hear though not see the ceremony.

Not all of my father's weddings came from over the Massachusetts line and not all of them took place in the parsonage. Home weddings were still very much favored, and church weddings were always an event in the community.

Everything about church weddings delighted me—the flower-banked altar, the ribbon-festooned pew ends, the romantic music, the bride and her attendants in their satins and laces, the flower girls strewing fragrant blossoms from their baskets. Two church weddings I especially remember. One was a military wedding where the West Point bridegroom and his bride left the church under a shining arch of classmates' high-held swords.

The other church wedding was memorable in a very different way. The bride's father, who was to give his daughter away, was a notorious periodic drinker and the day before the wedding he disappeared and could not be found anywhere. His daughter was nearly frantic. My father advised the couple to go ahead bravely and without explanation, and so the bride, lovely but pale, came to the altar on the arm of an uncle. In the middle of the ceremony the guests heard a slight commotion in the vestibule and, turning, saw the bride's father, impeccably groomed but bleary of eye and uncertain of step, making dignified although rather wobbly progress down the aisle. My father, sizing up the situation, silently beckoned him to a place behind the bride and, though the uncle had already given her away, asked him, "Who giveth this woman to be married to this man?" The bride's father, acquainted with the role by reason of rehearsals, declared without hesitation, "*I* do," then swayed into a seat made vacant for him in the front pew. The ceremony went on and soon the triumphal march pealed the twice-given-away bride and the tense-faced bridegroom down the aisle.

One summer when my mother was away for a few days and my father and I were keeping house together, a couple arrived in the early evening wanting to be married. Father sent me across the street to find a second witness and soon a neighbor and I were in our parlor with the waiting pair. It was beginning to grow dark so I lighted the parlor lamp. Suddenly I remembered that I had neglected to fill the lamps since Mother had left. I prayed hard that there might be enough oil in this one to see us through the service, but right in the middle of the ceremony its light began to flicker. For a moment or two the flame fluttered vaguely; it grew dim, then went out altogether.

My father did not stop or even hesitate. Paying no attention to the lack of light he went on, reciting the service from memory. As he began the concluding prayer I tiptoed out, fumbled my way down the dark back stairs to the cellar where the big kerosene can was kept, dragged it up the stairs to the kitchen, and by the waning light in the western sky hastily filled a lamp. Taking it into the parlor I set it on the table beside the useless parlor lamp.

Everyone politely ignored the incident, but when we were alone my father chided me—mildly, for he could see that I felt badly disgraced. I was not particularly troubled by the strange memory the bridal couple would have of their marriage or by my own lack of responsibility. It was what the neighbor might think that bothered me most, and what she might tell others about the state of things at the parsonage when the minister's wife was away. For months whenever I met this neighbor I blushed at the recollection of the unfilled parlor lamp.

My father believed wholeheartedly in lifelong marriages. He gave wise counsel to couples whose marriage seemed about to go on the rocks and was deeply distressed if it finally broke up. As a general rule he did not approve of divorce, but neither did he believe in depriving a man whose wife had left him, or a woman whose husband had deserted her or was perpetually drunk and abusive, of the chance of a happier second marriage. Always before marrying anyone who had been divorced he insisted on a private conference with him or her and sometimes would refuse to perform the ceremony.

Occasionally a bridegroom would come to him to try to persuade him to falsify the date on the marriage certificate because the girl was pregnant. The date on the license on file at the town hall did not worry the couple; what concerned them was the date on the certificate which they would have in their home and be expected to show to their friends. Needless to say my father never cooperated in any such deception.

The difference in Massachusetts and Connecticut marriage laws ceased to exist a few years after we moved to the town just south of the Massachusetts—Connecticut line, when the Connecticut legislature passed a law also requiring a five-day interval between license and marriage. Massachusetts couples who made up their minds in a hurry could no longer rush into Connecticut and be married, and so the era of unscheduled weddings in our parsonage home came to an end.

The weeks just before the enactment of the restrictive Connecticut law saw a rush of Massachusetts young people coming over the border to be married. One day my father was called to the town hall to marry three couples there, and later that same day he married another pair in the parsonage. Twice he recorded having three marriages at home in a single day, and on several occasions, two.

Two hours before the midnight when the Connecticut law was

159

to go into effect there was a ring at our door. My father answered and found a burly policeman standing there with a timid couple in tow. He propelled them gently toward the opened door. "I found 'em roamin' the streets lookin' for a parson," he said grinning. "Better tie 'em up proper!"

18. A Liberal Education

High school did not fill me with enthusiasm. It was something I accepted as part of the daily routine, doing whatever studying was necessry to receive passing grades but not much more. English and history classes I enjoyed; Latin, French, and science courses were a hardship and a bore.

My father, disturbed by my lack of interest in Latin, offered to tutor me. His method was to glance at my next day's assignment in Caesar's *Commentaries* and quickly translate it aloud. Part of this I jotted down; the rest I more or less memorized, making no attempt to understand the grammatical construction. My mother protested this procedure, but it went on practically the whole year. The next year, completely incapable of conquering Cicero, I abandoned Latin, much to my father's disappointment. He overlooked the fact that it was partly his fault and offered to teach me Greek, which he said I would find more interesting than

Latin. We started out enthusiastically but soon gave up the project for lack of time.

My English assignments were no problem, even when the teacher began requiring daily themes. Some of my classmates found this difficult, and when a couple of boys asked me for help I willingly wrote a few paragraphs which they copied and handed in as their own. Of course the teacher soon detected the deception and pinned it on me. She lectured me severely about the unethical aspect of what I had done and put an end to it. Somehow I had not associated it with wrongdoing; I was just being helpful—and enjoying the popularity it gave me with the boys. When with the end of the arrangement this waned, my friend Peggy remarked, "They were just using you. Boys don't like smart girls." I hadn't aspired to being smart; I would have preferred being popular, as she was.

The books I borrowed from the small public library interested me more than my textbooks. For the most part my parents let my choice of books go unchallenged, but once in awhile my mother would glance over the books I brought home. *Huckleberry Finn* she asked me not to read, because it was "vulgar." She also objected to Margaret Deland's stories, because they "were concerned with problems too adult for me as yet." Of course this whetted my curiosity and I finished them standing up among the library bookshelves since there was no reading room. My father encouraged my enthusiasm for books. If he were within hearing when Mother called me from my reading to do some household task he would plead, "Oh, let her read!"

Mother would have been glad for me to take more interest in needlework, as Helen had always done. Returning from a visit to relatives in New Jersey she told me that a cousin only a little older than I was doing some beautiful embroidery. "She asked me," Mother said, "if Edith did much fancy work, and I had to tell her that Edith had her nose in a book much oftener than she had a needle in her hand."

Not to be outdone by this much-approved-of cousin, and because a high-school talent show was coming up with an exhibition of all kinds of student handicrafts, including needlework, I stirred myself and picked up crochet hook and needle. Within a fairly short time I produced a crocheted bag, a Mexican drawnwork doily, and an embroidered pillowtop—all of which were displayed at the talent show. I had not disliked making them, but I had missed my reading and with these accomplishments to my credit I went back to it.

Besides borrowing books from the town library I read many from my father's shelves. Although mostly religious in character they held a good selection of the classics and some more modern works, most of them gifts from relatives or friends who knew Father's fondness for books. Fiction was poorly represented, but there were a few Dickens titles and a complete set of George Eliot. I found the long passages of moralistic preaching in her novels boring but read them conscientiously because Father said that skipping was discourteous to the author. When we were reading aloud Hugo's *Les Miserables* and wanted to omit the long description of the Battle of Waterloo Father would not allow it; every word of it must be read. What was more, he seemed to enjoy it.

Curiously too, in view of his passion for peace, Creasey's *Fifteen Decisive Battles of the World* was one of his favorite books. I suppose his interest lay in the strategies employed and the logistics involved. I remember his marking out for us on a sandy beach the battle position of an ancient phalanx, and he expounded the same thing after we had seen the Connecticut governor's footguard, called the Israel Putnam Phalanx, take part in a parade.

This happened when I was still in grammar school as part of a three-day celebration in Hartford on the completion of a fine new bridge across the Connecticut River. My father convinced Mother that he should take Helen, then in high school, and me to see this parade. The historical floats and the marching organizations would be something we would not forget; we would, he was sure, learn more from them than from a day in school. So he and Helen and I rode to Hartford on crowded trolleys and stood on street curbs for hours watching the parade go by. Altogether, we had an exciting day, but Father was much disappointed that the Israel Putnam Phalanx was to march the next day instead of that one. Insisting that we must return to see it, he overrode Mother's veto and took us back to see the brilliant company march, then supplied us with ample information on the place of the phalanx in ancient times.

My classmates were envious and my teacher disapproving of my two-day absence from school. Mother, also disapproving, made

Father write the customary excuse for me to carry to my teacher. In his note he stated his belief that occasionally outside events could contribute as much to one's education as school studies. My teacher, making the punishment fit the crime, required me to write a composition on what I had learned during my two days' absence.

Unlike me, Father was a poor customer of the public library. He was a slow and thoughtful reader and wanted to own his books so he could underscore passages, make marginal comments, and have the books at hand to refer to or to reread if the spirit so moved. He and I disagreed completely about his belief that "any book worth reading is worth rereading."

In one community where we lived, one of the town physicians was a former college classmate of my father. The two men were congenial companions, sharing many of the same interests. They frequently went to lectures at the nearby college and each year attended together the area's Williams College alumni dinner. On one occasion they both wanted to read a certain book and since it was quite expensive they agreed to buy it jointly. It was not a satisfactory arrangement. Both men were slow readers; both wanted to mark pages but did not dare because of the other half-owner; both wanted to keep the book. Which one finally got it I don't remember, but I do recall my father grumbling, "Better no book at all than half a book." The experiment was not repeated.

Always eager to add to his library, Father reacted with enthusiasm when a periodical to which he subscribed offered an up-to-date set of encyclopedias free with an extended renewal. He read aloud the glamorous prospectus and we all became excited about this major book acquisition. When he was notified that a box was waiting for him at the express office he borrowed the next-door youngster's cart to drag the heavy book box home. On his return we saw in the cart a package about the size of three fat books. We watched curiously as Father opened the box and took out the much-touted encyclopedia set. It was, to be sure, complete in the specified number of volumes—but such small volumes! Reexamining the prospectus we discovered that the size of the books was nowhere mentioned. It was our wishful thinking that had magnified them to Britannica size! Annoyed at first, we soon began to see it all as a good joke on Father and the rest of us.

Beauty of language, especially in poetry, always touched a responsive chord in Father. He was quick to distinguish between the real and the phony and was not likely to be taken in by the pretentious, the ponderous, or the sentimental. The music of poetry was alive to him, and any lilting line stamped itself on his memory almost automatically. He could quote long passages from Wordsworth and Tennyson and Burns, who were among his favorite poets. Often he would recite a few lines, effortlessly and effectively, to bring out some point in a sermon. Never, I think, did he consciously memorize a verse for this purpose; he just drew on his seemingly inexhaustible inner treasury.

Father thought the "new poetry" then coming into fashion affected and unmusical. One year he attended a ministers' meeting in Boston at which Amy Lowell gave a reading from her poems. "It wasn't poetry at all," Father told us on his return, and he proceeded to recite a poem Miss Lowell had read—and which he had heard only that once—complete with her inflection and mannerisms. "Now compare that with this," he said, and with considerably more sympathy he recited one of Wordsworth's poems on the same subject.

Yet his fondness for what he considered real poetry did not prevent his enjoying doggerel and even inventing it himself for some special occasion. He was always ready to liven up a church social with some such humorous narrative poem as "John Gilpin's Ride" or "The One-Hoss Shay." Occasionally he would come forth with a poem we had never heard before and when we asked in surprise, "Where did you get that one?" he would answer with almost equal surprise, "Why, I really don't know. It just popped into my head. Hadn't thought of it for years."

In contrast to my father, my mother had never, she said, been able to memorize anything. She compared herself to the minister who told his congregation that the only hymn he really knew was "I Have a Charge to Keep." She thought she knew one poem— "Abou Ben Adam"—but like as not when she tried to recite it she would flounder and Father would come to her rescue. "Well, anyhow," Mother would defend herself, "I know the sense of it even if I don't remember the exact words." To "know the sense" of a thing was what she considered important. All the children of the family seemed to take after her in this respect; not one of us inherited Father's gift of laying hold on anything with a poetic flavor and possessing it forevermore. Was it perhaps a happy legacy from some remote Celtic ancestor transmitted to him through his Scotch-Irish father?

My parents were quick to take advantage of cultural events in the community or nearby environs, both for themselves and for their children. We heard lectures on such burning issues as socialism, temperance, woman's suffrage, "The Negro in America," as well as stereopticon lectures on such remote places as Venice, Palestine, Africa, and Alaska. In Springfield we saw and heard such noted persons as Helen Keller and Dr. Grenfell of Labrador. Mother made a point of joining the Women's Club wherever we lived and of going to its literary programs. When we lived near Wesleyan College while my brothers were attending it we all went fairly frequently to evening lectures there and to intercollegiate debates. In those days before radio and TV, we found those contests quite exciting. And of course we never missed such extraordinary events as the appearance at the college of President Taft for the installation of a new college president.

Few musical opportunities were available to us—an occasional concert featuring a singer, a pianist, or a violinist, once a band of bell ringers, and once a chorus of black Jubilee singers. One of our neighbors bought an exceptionally fine Victrola and invited us in sometimes to hear a few excellent records. But I was eighteen before I heard my first live symphony.

We were made conscious of our New England heritage by visits to historical and literary landmarks. Two or three times my father and I spent a day together in Hartford for the express purpose of absorbing its historical atmosphere. In the senate chamber of the capitol I sat in the presiding senator's chair made from the wood of the famed Charter Oak and at the state library I saw the original charter that was hidden in that tree. Once Mother and I put in several days in Boston "seeing the sights," mostly historical, and when Father joined us we toured the Harvard buildings in Cambridge, then went on to Mt. Auburn Cemetery to see the burial place of many of New England's illustrious dead.

From the ministerial meetings of the area, which Father attended faithfully, he gained much from papers and discussions on cultural and civic as well as religious subjects. Not infrequently Father presented a paper; one he mentioned in his journal was entitled: "Christ as the Thinking Christian's Master." At least one year he was program chairman of the district Preachers' Association and for many years he was a member of two important Conference committees—Conference Claimants, deciding on pensions for retired ministers, and the committee which examined young men applying for admission to the Conference.

On his return from his trips to these gatherings Father would share with us his interesting experiences, his meeting with persons in different lines of work and their opinions on business matters, educational practices, or civic affairs. When, as happened several times, he went to Washington or New York he managed to include much strenuous sightseeing—which he made dramatically real to us at home. Once, before I was born, he journeyed as far west as Chicago to visit the World's Fair in progress there at that time and on the way back stopped off at Niagara Falls. This trip was the high point, travelwise, of his life. Most of his knowledge, he would have been the first to admit, came from people and things close at hand and from his reading.

By the time I was in grammar school and all during my high-school days Father and I had a little routine which we practiced several times a week on the pretext of saving his eyes. While I read aloud to him he would shave, making it a long chore. Having delayed it until my return from school (unless he had been obliged to go out in the morning) he would hang up a great strap—a strop—near the wall mirror in the kitchen, put a little tin of water on the stove to heat, and tuck a towel under his chin. While I read aloud he would sharpen the edge of his long-bladed razor by stroking it up and down on the strop, every now and then holding the razor up to inspect its edge. At the same time he might remark, "That last paragraph was especially fine. Read it again, will you?"

He encouraged my interruptions, and we discussed together the essays of Emerson and of Carlyle which he had chosen for reading. The hot water in the shaving mug would grow cold and more would have to be heated, and the lather on Father's face would harden as we talked. Razor in hand he would pause to listen more intently or to ponder one of my questions. Always he tried to answer them as fully as possible, treating me as an intelligent person and his equal in understanding.

Once I advanced a theory which irritated him into saying, "You need a better grounding in theology. You should read some of the books I studied in theological seminary."

When I asked impertinently, "Were they written twenty-five years before then?" he got the point.

"No," he answered thoughtfully, "I guess they weren't." And he never again suggested my reading books he had studied in the 1880's.

"John!" Mother would call from the next room. "Do get on with your shaving. At this rate you won't get started on your calls before dark. And Edith should be doing her homework."

My father and I would look at each other like a couple of conspirators. "Just one more page," he would plead. For a moment or two he would speed up his shaving, then lapse into the contemplative mood so much a part of these sessions. Neither Mother nor I realized it—nor perhaps my father—but I was getting from them a more liberal education than any amount of homework could give me.

When we were reading *Ivanhoe* in school Father asked me how I liked it. "Oh, it's not so much," I replied airily. "I could write about as well as that myself."

Father looked at me gravely. "In that case," he said, "you'd better begin right now." And he handed me a pencil and a piece of paper.

Yet he did not mean to ridicule or belittle any literary aspirations I might have. He was pleased when, as a high-school senior, my English teacher asked me to correct freshman papers for her—at the munificent sum of twenty-five cents an hour. And when on graduation I won two statewide essay contests both he and Mother were as delighted as I.

When we studied Burns in our English literature course I asked Father, who was a great admirer of the Scottish poet and knew dozens of his poems, a question which really puzzled me. "How do you reconcile your love of Burns's poetry with your knowledge of his personal life?" Here, I thought, would be an argument worth having!

Without a moment's hesitation my father replied simply, "I don't."

My mouth opened in surprise. Gone was the argument I had expected. I wondered if I would ever understand this father of mine—a man so "set" in so many ways yet quick to admit his contradictory feelings. When he was invited to be the speaker at the local Burns Society annual dinner I was proud, but I could not help wondering if some of the people there might not have my question in their minds.

Many of my classmates were planning after high-school graduation to attend one of the several state normal schools and then to become teachers. This rather appealed to me, and my mother, having herself been a teacher, encouraged me in such a future. The two-year normal-school course would, I knew, be much less of a financial strain on my parents than a four-year college course. And I had to admit that I had not done well enough in high school, except in English and history, to warrant the sacrifice a college course would mean.

Herbert, my second brother, after teaching in an out-of-state high school, was now at Yale on a fellowship, studying for his doctor's degree preparatory to college teaching. On a visit home he dropped a bombshell. "Why should Edie be a teacher?" he asked. "She likes books; why shouldn't she become a librarian? It's a growing profession and I think she'd enjoy it. At least let her look into it."

A little earlier the town, long aware that its library was disgracefully inadequate, had held a town meeting at which it accepted Mr. Carnegie's offer of a new library building. This was nearing completion only a block away from the parsonage, and a young woman trained in the Springfield library apprentice course had been engaged as librarian. A couple of lesser places were open to applicants, and after an interview I was taken on as an assistant. I was to work for three months without pay, then for a dollar a day (the hours two to nine) four days a week.

Soon after finishing high school I began my work at the library. I liked everything about it, even mending old books. Best of all were the after-school hours when I helped the children select their books. Now I was sure which way my path to the future led.

I helped swell the new library's circulation by taking home armfuls of books, and in my free mornings began to study for the three-day entrance examinations into a qualified library school. I went back to high school for a course in German, since a second modern language was required, and at home I read, read, read. Eagerly I looked forward to the liberal education which lay ahead, but not for years did I appreciate how firmly it was based on the liberal education already acquired in my parsonage home.

19. For Goodness' Sake!

"The King of Love My Shepherd Is, Whose Goodness Faileth Never" my father sang as he walked about the house or hoed in the garden or chopped stove-sized logs at the woodpile. He believed it too. All around him he saw the evidence of God's goodness. So, I'm sure, did Mother, but in a rather more prosaic way. Father saw it constantly in the beauty of nature, to which he was ever responsive, and in the beauty of language, especially in the Bible, classical prose, and fine poetry. He also interpreted goodness as happy family life and as harmonious relationships among the nations and races of mankind. Neither he nor Mother had any racial prejudices, and Father would welcome a black man into his pulpit or study or at his table as cordially as a white one. His mission in life was to help make God's goodness prevail on earth among all men. "My aim," he wrote in his journal, "is to promote the kingdom."

Righteous conduct—judged, as was natural, by his own strict standards—was the way he believed men should acknowledge God's goodness, contribute to it, and repay it. It was man who had caused the evils of the world by his waywardness, his alienation from God, and his "inhumanity to man." By continually pointing out the goodness of God, and by his own upright example, Father tried to influence men and women toward righteousness.

Goodness and *good* were words often on my father's lips. A *good* day, a *good* man, a *good* meeting, a *good* congregation, a *good* sermon (someone else's). He liked to recite the twenty-seventh psalm that extols "the goodness of the Lord in the land of the living," and the psalms beginning: "O give thanks to the Lord for he is good." Above all he cherished the twenty-third psalm with its "Surely goodness and mercy shall follow me all the days of my life, and I shall dwell in the house of the Lord forever."

Among Father's sermon texts his journal records: "And God saw that it was good" (Genesis 1:10); "The hand of our God is upon all them for good that seek him" (Ezra 8:22); and for the last Sunday of December: "Thou crownest the year with thy goodness" (Psalm 65:11).

"Let us praise the Lord in song for his goodness," Father would often say in announcing a joyful hymn to begin the "praise service" which often preceded a prayer meeting. He emphasized the happiness of life and called for more joy in religion. "Be of good cheer, brethren," he would say. "Being good does not mean going about with a long face. Remember, God giveth the sun!"

Father had a fine sense of humor and he could take a joke, even on himself. He let us twit him about his occasional absent-mindedness and even laughed with us when Mother asked him to fill the teakettle on the stove and he drew a dipperful of water from the tap, then proceed to pour it into the coal hod standing on the floor beside the stove.

My mother's funnybone was not so pronounced; her attempt at jokes often did not " come off," and she sometimes found it difficult to appreciate the constant flow of wit and attempted wit with which she was surrounded. When things became a little too hilarious she would try to calm us down with "Fun's fun, children, but it mustn't go too far." Life was to her a serious matter and one not to be taken too lightly.

Language, like fun, must stay within bounds in our household. For instance, the expression "For Heaven's sake!" was outlawed as being too close to swearing. Instead we might say "For goodness' sake!" This might even help us to remember what we were all striving for, not only for ourselves as individuals but in order to provide good examples for others.

This Example business I felt Father sometimes carried too far. One summer the whole town was upset by the drowning of two young men while they were out canoeing on the river on a Sunday afternoon. At the funeral service, which Father conducted, he spoke of the tragedy as being doubly painful because of its having occurred on the Lord's Day. He reminded his listeners of the command: "Remember the Sabbath Day to keep it holy," and he pled with them not to follow this unhappy example of Sabbath-breaking—lest, he seemed to imply, they too incur God's wrath and punishment.

I was badly shaken by Father's talk. It seemed to me all wrong. Why, I asked my mother, had Father preached a sermon against breaking the Sabbath? Why hadn't he shown the warm, human side of his nature by expressing his grief and his sympathy?

"Don't think your father was not deeply distressed by this tragedy," Mother said. "He did not want to do what he did, but after much prayer he felt that as a good pastor it was his duty to try to turn this bad example to some good purpose." And she added that he had obtained the consent of both families to speak as he had. She persuaded me not to mention the matter to my father; my reaction, she said, would not help anything and would only disturb him. So I kept silent about it, but it continued to bother me.

My mother was too much of an individual not to make her own contribution in the struggle to bring about a world where goodness would prevail. She chose the temperance field as her special area of endeavor. Why this reform especially appealed to her I have no idea; no one in her family had ever, to my knowledge, succumbed to the bottle. Her work began in her home, sharing with her children items in the papers and tracts of the Women's Christian Temperance Union, which came in regularly. We heard and read stories about the evil effects of drink, the wickedness of saloons, the plight of children clothed in rags because of their fathers' addiction to liquor. We saw countless cartoons of drunkards in gutters and snakes in whisky bottles, and we learned temperance songs, including one beginning: "Look not on the ruby wine/ Sparkling in its beauty."

Mother's feeling against alcohol went so far as to forbid us children to drink root beer or ginger ale. Being told that they were not alcoholic did not change her mind. Their names alone, she insisted, were enough to condemn them. Water was always the best drink, though lemonade was pleasant in summer and orange "pop" was permissible.

While her children were small, Mother's activities in connection with the temperance fight were confined to the local arena. She attended W.C.T.U. meetings regularly, often contributing to their programs. Temperance Sunday, she saw to it, was well observed in our church, not only in Sunday school but in Junior League and Epworth League meetings. And she frequently persuaded Father to invite a temperance speaker to occupy his pulpit on this day. Every fall she organized a W.C.T.U. sponsored reception for public-school teachers, with music and refreshments and a speaker who would emphasize the bad effects of alcohol on the human system. (This information, it was thought, might be included in physiology lessons.)

When I was in high school and the only one of the children left at home, Mother expanded her W.C.T.U. activities. She began to accept invitations in neighboring communities and then farther afield to speak at temperance gatherings, to help organize local "unions," to judge young people's temperance speaking contests and award prizes for the winning temperance essays. She served as local or county delegate at state W.C.T.U. conventions and once went as Hartford County delegate to the national convention at Portland, Oregon, on her return reporting the meetings all over the state. Mother enjoyed everything about these expeditions—the traveling, the meetings, the new friends, and the presentation of her reports.

Father was sympathetic with Mother's involvement in the temperance struggle. When the local-option issue was to be voted on in the fall election, determining whether or not the town would have open saloons, he helped organize evening rallies which were held in large halls in order to attract non-churchgoers, and were addressed by some high-powered speaker from out of town. To my

173

parents' disappointment the no-license vote always lost on election day, though sometimes by a fairly narrow margin, and the saloons continued to flourish.

Mother's W.C.T.U. reports and correspondence, as well as her letters to friends and relatives and of course to the four children away from home, made it necessary for her to spend a good deal of time at her desk. She was pleased that the boys and Helen answered her letters rather regularly; these letters were read aloud for Father and me to enjoy too. We were all delighted when one of them would arrive, sometimes unannounced, for a weekend or to spend a few days of vacation time.

The times when Mother was away and Father and I kept house together at home increased the sense of companionship he and I had always felt. We read, talked, walked, and played checkers together. I enjoyed being in charge of running the house, especially of buying supplies and planning and preparing meals. One reason I liked this was that I was allowed to keep anything I could save out of the limited food budget I was given. At first I was inclined to be overthrifty, but at Father's insistence soon learned to depend less on rice, macaroni, and beans. Usually I stuck to familiar dishes but occasionally experimented with new recipes. These, my father labeled "Edith's concoctions," and often announced his preference for applesauce, though he was always pleasant about it. Once, when I served some not-too-light biscuits, he remarked, "Are you perhaps expecting an enemy invasion and preparing ammunition?"

One day I heard Father coming hurriedly down the stairs. "Do you have any idea how to take out an ink stain?" he asked. "I've just pushed an open ink bottle off my desk." This was serious, for the church-owned study carpet was light-colored. I remembered seeing Mother take out an ink spot by using sour milk. Finding we had some of this, we took it upstairs along with old cloths and a brush. Blotters Father had thrown on had absorbed much of the fresh ink, and by repeated applications of the milk, together with much scrubbing and rinsing, we were able to minimize the damage. Father's turning to me for help, our working together on the difficult job, and his expressing his appreciation—as one adult to another—all meant much to me.

Mother was not much of a walker, and I was frequently my father's companion on the long walks he enjoyed taking. One walk he especially liked was down a broad, elm-edged road to where, a mile from the parsonage, a pillared, white-spired, Congregational church stood. I often made this walk with him after the Sunday evening service. He was relaxed then, and in a mood to talk. If the night were clear and the sky star-filled, he would point out various constellations and tell me their names and the Greek legends connected with them. Very likely he would also recite an appropriate poem or two.

When we reached a point opposite the white church we would pause to rest a moment before turning back. Father would gaze across the wide street at the church which, he told me, stood on the site of an earlier one where the Calvinist theologian Jonathan Edwards had preached more than once. It was there, said Father, that Edwards had preached his famous sermon "Sinners in the Hands of an Angry God," and preached so powerfully that men had "clung to the pillars to keep from sliding into hell."

In Father's voice I seemed to detect a note of admiration and perhaps even a tinge of envy of this man whose preaching swayed his hearers so tremendously. "The God whom Jonathan Edwards preached," Father said simply, "was a great God!"

The depth of Father's belief in his religion and his dedication to it did not diminish with the years. This was apparent to my brother Rob and me when, one summer after I had left home, he and I happened to be visiting there at the same time. With Mother we attended a Sunday evening service; the subject of Father's talk was Jesus' miracle of turning the water into wine. It was during prohibition days, and while eating a snack at home after the service my brother and I commented facetiously on the popularity this miracle would have brought Jesus in certain circles in our time. We even speculated on the possible social and economic effects of such a talent.

Suddenly my father rose, his face white with suppressed emotion. He bade us stop our talk, saying, "You may make fun of me all you like, but I cannot allow you to ridicule my religion." And he strode to his study, closing the door behind him.

My brother and I were appalled. We had only been having a little fun, without the least intention of being disrespectful either to our father or to his religion. Singly Rob and I rapped on the study door, were admitted, and apologized. Soon everything was as before. But not quite. Both Rob and I realized as we had not done fully before how wholeheartedly Father believed in the miracles of Jesus and how to him—as we remembered having heard him say— Jesus was as real as the people about him.

Already, during my last years at home before going away to school and despite differing viewpoints, I was gaining a better understanding of the essential values which governed and guided my parents' lives. Mine, I began to realize, might be different, but they would never cease to be influenced by the high ideals, the constant striving for goodness that had been held up to me by them. Not the pursuit of happiness but the pursuit of goodness was the overriding aim of my parents' lives. Happiness, they believed, was not something to seek but a gift of God to be accepted gratefully as a by-product of the good life.

My brothers declared that in our home on the wall above the dining-room table there hung a framed motto: "God Bless Our Home," and that over it was draped a frequently used twig switch. This I do not remember, and my mother denied the story altogether. I could more easily believe that the most completely appropriate family motto, even with a twig switch above it, would have read: "For Goodness' Sake!"